Contents

Cover Design and interior layout: Jeremy Holden (JeremyHolden.me)

Editing Team: Tammy Roach, Nancy Sheridan

Graphic Design by BK Design Solutions www.bkdesignsolutions.com

BALANCE
The GAMEPLAN
to **FINDING TIME** for your
YOUNG LIVING BUSINESS
with

It's 4:57 a.m.

I n a little less than three minutes, the microphone will go live, and my voice will go out to seven million people in the city of Chicago — those just waking up, those who have started their morning commute into work, those shuttling their kids onto school buses and those beginning their day. Twenty seconds ago, I was on the phone with a U.S. Senator, getting feedback on a story that would headline the morning. I have just a few seconds to grab one soundbite, work it into my newscast, and be ready to hit the airwaves with no mistakes.

It's a dance, the clock and me. We are enemies. Every second in a newsroom is critical. There is neither time to eat, nor time for water. There are no breaks in my shift. It is only stress. It is like that for every news anchor at every radio station in the country. My fingers fly over the keyboard as I proofread what I have written. It's 4:59. I have 25 seconds until go time. It needs to be perfect —delivered with accuracy, the right intonation and inflection and pause, powerful words, concise and to time. I have 30 seconds to tell the story. To be an anchor, you need to write concisely and deliver the words with authority. Less is more.

Then I hear the stinger go off — my musical cue that it's time to turn on the microphone. My board lights up. My heart races. For a split second, I have butterflies and feel a little lightheaded at the power that is trusted to me to be a source of reliability. To be credible. To be honest. To be balanced. To be fair. And with no time to adjust to my emotions, off I go, seamlessly into another newscast. I must be fearless. I have delivered over 40-thousand newscasts over my career in Chicago and upstate New York. I read the script before me from top to bottom, every word so carefully chosen as I race the clock to the end of the script. It must be flawless. It must time out exactly to the second. There can be no errors. I have only one shot to get it right. And that chance is taken before a live audience.

The thrill of the performance and the size of the crowd makes my adrenaline race. I get closer and closer to the bottom of the script — the soundbite plays over the air, the one I spent an hour hunting down and editing. The last words are read. The lights go off. There is silence. And it's just me, my microphone, and 25 more minutes to write the next newscast. The old newscast is tossed away, never to be used again. And I start the next race against time. It's the thrill of the news hunt for content and tape, and the never-ending pain of the relentless, ticking clock.

I read 39 newspapers each shift to cover every geographic area the radio waves hit; and I write about 60 stories by hand, alone. It is grueling, difficult work as I wrestle with the language and fight with the clock. But then there is release. It's over. I can breathe. I realize I've not had food for a third of the day. When you are in that chair, you think of nothing but preparation and the time on the clock. I grab my coat, get into the elevator and in a few moments am out into the Chicago air, looking for my car in a parking garage. I slip into invisibility on the street. Now, I am mom.

I start the 72-mile drive home to my five kids. I have worked the overnight shift in Chicago for 11 years, so my husband can carry a 9 to 5 job and one of us is home during the day with our children, who are 0, 2, 4, 6, and 8. I am on the radio with personalities making millions of dollars a year. But the average network news anchor in radio in the 90's takes home only $35,000 a year to start. Half my paycheck goes into my gas tank, to park my car, and for tolls to get to work every single day. Our family of seven is living on $16,000 a year. It's poverty level. We live in the projects. We get aid for our heat and our food and our medical care. But no one at work knows.

I let my mind wander into all the responsibilities of my day: my eight-year-old's free Judo lesson at the YMCA at 3 p.m., no groceries in the cupboards, an overdue electric bill, and six hours of homeschooling ahead — and I start to nod off behind the wheel. It's a regular occurrence for me, highway hypnosis, as I navigate the long drive back to my home five or six days a week, completely exhausted. I have absolutely nothing left to give. I feel the grid marks on the highway loudly snap me back into reality as I swerve slightly to the right side of the road, my body, not wanting to go anymore.

I relent in my fight for rest and pull over at a gas station o take a 20-minute catnap. If I sleep for 30 minutes, my husband will be late for work. I get just enough rest to make my body go a little further — to keep me alert for the last 20 miles of the drive. I stumble into my home a few minutes before 9 a.m., the kids running up to me, rested, excited, and ready for another day — and plant a kiss on my husband's cheek as he runs out the door.

This is my life. Work, kids, work, kids — and no relief. No break. No way out. No reprieve. This is how I lived for 36 straight years. 12 of them were in the government projects.

I snap back into reality. My kids are hungry.

I open the cabinets to see if there's anything I can feed them, but they are empty. There is nothing. The milk is gone, inside, there are just a few odds and ends that don't amount to a full meal of anything — and I have five little blue-eyed towheaded kids looking up at me, waiting for nourishment. I get their coats and mittens on, remembering that this is food pantry day. We all pile into the family van and drive a few miles away to wait in a 3-hour line in 30-degree temperatures. The van is cold and has no heat for the drive because my blower fan is out. But I am thankful because it runs. Last year, we went through six transmissions in four used cars in six months. If my engine runs and I can get to work, heat is not mandatory. Every two weeks I have to make the choice of taking my check and fixing my van or putting gasoline in it so I can get to work and keep my job. The gasoline wins.

By the time we make it to the front of the food pantry line, the bread and soup is gone. I ask if they have any meat. There hasn't been meat for three weeks. All that was left was chocolate pudding. We leave with three grocery bags full of chocolate pudding. We go home and eat it twice that day, then again the next day, and the next, until our food stamps go through.

I'm at my lowest of the low. I feel like I cannot do anything right. The kids are irritable and fighting. They press my patience. The school day is long and bland as my body begs for a nap. I want to be the mom that puts my kids in the van and takes them to amazing places that we study. I want to be the mom that breaks out art projects and teaches my kids foreign languages and grows tadpoles for science class, but I have nothing left to give them. I want to be the mom that goes on bike rides with my kids and plays Legos on the floor with them. But all my energy was left in the anchor chair. The juggle to be mom, work full time, teach them, and pay the bills was more than my plate could carry. I was dropping it all. I was mediocre at everything, and a master of nothing. Every day was a race to not make a mistake. I wanted more time for my husband, more time to take care of my body, more time to rest. I wanted more time to cook better food.

My kids trusted me, and we were eating processed chocolate pudding. They knew I would take care of them, yet I knew our power was set to be shut off that day. We didn't have enough in our bank account to keep it on, which meant we'd have to wear our jackets to bed until my next check cleared — unless I wrote a bad check and prayed it didn't bounce before my paycheck was deposited. We had nowhere to turn.

I couldn't work harder. I already had a full-time job, homeschooling and a special-needs son. My husband had a full-time job and college, too. But he was making a few dollars over minimum wage while he finished his degree. And my check wasn't enough to survive. How do you dig out when you have no hope? How do you juggle it all when there are more plates than you have hands? How do you find time to take care of things that are so very important — your body, your marriage, your faith — when you're in survival mode every moment?

> I had no idea in that very first class where all of this would lead.

We lived in the projects without enough food, sometimes without power, and always operating under extreme stress. My husband and I both graduated from college and moved across the country, away from the projects, and took white collar jobs in 2007. But we were still just surviving. We now had $70,000 in student loans. A mortgage. Two vehicle payments. Credit card debt. And it seemed everything we saved was gone immediately in the next emergency.

Fast forward another seven years. I was sitting in my first Young Living Essential oils class. I wish I knew then what I know now! I wish I knew prosperity and freedom were on the other side of the starter kit. I wish I knew when I was hungry and tired and beaten down that if I kept walking a few more steps, there was release, if only I could manage my clock and find balance. If only I could be disciplined. If only I could find the time. If only I could push my weary body a bit more. I had no idea in that very first class where all of this would lead. It was just a kit. It was just a box of oils.

I was an accidental business builder with Young Living, because I never thought I had enough time. I started sharing oils simply because I could not afford them and I needed them for free, not because I had a solid business strategy. In my head when I first began, the business was an impossibility because I simply could not pile one more thing on top of five kids and my job. I was the one no one would ever spot to work the business on their team. I was the always-busy mom. I was the overworked employee. I was the thirty-something that was adrenally burned out. I had no hope and no future, just more years of juggling nothing and dropping everything. If you could predict a leader that would explode on your team, it would not have been me. I was frazzled, fried and weary. I was the one no one asked.

How do you dig out from that place?? Is there truly no hope? Why did I stay in a place of survival mode for two decades? It's all I thought I was capable of. I had no discipline. I did not cast wide enough visions.

I'm here to tell you everything I thought was wrong.

I now believe in freedom for my family, and I believe in it for you. I get to tell you the rest of the story, and it's so much more fun than the beginning. It's a Cinderella story of renewal and change. But it all started with one word: Oola.

IT ALL STARTED WITH ONE WORD: Oola

What Is **Oola**, and Why Do I Need This Book?

Oola is simply a life that is balanced and growing in the seven key areas of health and well-being. It can be a noun or a verb. It can be a destination or a feeling. It can be as complex as a life growing in fitness, finance, family, field, faith, friends, and fun (the 7 F's of Oola), or as simple as a sunset, a quiet book on the beach, or a special moment with a child. It is that place we all shoot for in life.

My name is Sarah Harnisch, and I am a Young Living Diamond. It seems surreal, but I am the woman from the story. The average Diamond in Young Living makes over $39,000 a month, according to the 2016 Young Living income disclosure guide. It took two and a half years from my starter kit to my Diamondship, but I am now debt free. I am no longer hungry. My kids go to bed with real doors instead of sheets for doors; real walls instead of bookcases for walls. I have time to care for my body. I have as much sleep as I need. I own my clock and I dictate where my steps will go and how my talent will be used.

I am Oola.

But that was not how the story began. How do you get from where you are, to freedom? What is the strategy? How do you do the daily juggle? Is it possible?? How did the story turn around so quickly? I saw a goal. I set aside excuses and started to be disciplined with my life. I made little spaces for Young Living. And it grew into something so much bigger than I ever imagined it would. If you are in that place — battle weary and worn to the core, this book was written exactly for you. It was written for every word spoken that there is no time. That it can't be done. That the juggle is impossible. That the climb is too high.

I hear you, weary one. But I want you to know that you have it in you to make the climb, even if you feel that what you have to give is so very little. Those tiny bits can be collected into something amazing, if only you can manage the self-control to balance the plates you have in the air effectively. That's what this little book is all about: how to do this when you feel you have nothing to give. Because in truth, you do have something to give. You are a hope-bringer and a world-changer. But it all starts with your feet. And they only move if you have a vision, a gameplan, a little bit of fire to see it through, and a strategy to keep the plates spinning.

Not only am I going to train you how to use Oola to focus your business, I'm going to train you how to train your leaders to use this powerful tool as well. Because when we have balance, we have success. If our leaders capture the ability to balance as well, we have duplication,

> I want you to know that you have it in you to make the climb

which is the most powerful tool you have in your Young Living business. Why is this book different from every other time management book out there? Because I am a mom of five that built my Diamondship with a full-time job on my shoulders. I have walked that road you are on. I'll apply what I have learned in time directly to a Young Living business and intertwine core Oola values throughout the entire book. Oola is all about balance. Balance and time are sisters if you want to have a life that has a positive cadence to it. One of the most common questions I get when I speak is "how do you do it all?" Here's the answer: I don't. I do a little bit very often. I let perfection go. That's all it takes to rock this — little targeted moments. Moderation and consistency are VERY Oola.

The purpose of this book is to pair three things I love that were instrumental in my transformation: Oola, Young Living oils, and Gameplan business training. Gameplan has sold 1.5 million copies. It's the manual for growing a Young Living business. For the first time, we are marrying the two concepts together to help you find balance. That's what you'll find in this book. Strategy and balance in the seven areas of the Oola life, with direct tips for time management and growing your Young Living business with a full plate. Then I'll wrap up this mini book with two scripts: one for business leaders to train Oola products to their team to boost OGV *(organizational group volume)*, and a second script to train your leaders on discipline so they can build an Oola life, one that is balanced. It will help them order their day so they can get the most out of their Young Living businesses.

What happened with the rest of the story? How did I dig out? How did I go from weary to warrior? How did I learn to balance a 4 a.m. anchoring shift and five homeschooled kiddos with 288 oils classes? How did I build my business from the ground up, with no friend circle, no money, and no time? The full story is in the Gameplan book. But the nitty gritty is that by learning to balance the key areas of my life, I was able to squeeze enough time out of my day to carve out the tiny start of a Young Living business. That little bud in the ground became a Silver organization four months after my kit, Gold five months later, then Platinum, and finally Diamond two and a half years after that oils box showed up on my porch. How did I do it? A script, a kit and lots of time in front of new faces.

But how did I do it? How did I find the time?

Oola.

Let's master the 7 F's from the Oola book first, then we're going to turn everything you've ever learned about Oola upside down and look at it through a business lens.

The 7 F's of **Oola**

When your life is in Oola, you're in the zone. Everything seems to be going your way. It's like swimming with the current. You're covering maximum ground with minimal effort. It's like finding $20 in the couch, getting all green lights, receiving a Christmas bonus in July, having all tweets re-tweeted, easily-slipping-into-your-skinny-jeans-good.

Each *"F"* represents a key area in life. Ask yourself as you read which areas where you are strong, and which areas where you are weak. Troy and Dave have even designed a quick quiz you can do to give yourself a solid evaluation of all seven areas.

Before we jump in, let's get to the OolaGuys. Who are they??! They wrote a book that hit the international bestseller charts called *Oola: Find Balance in an Unbalanced World.* Gary and Mary Young, the founders of the 1.5-billion-dollar Young Living Essential Oils company, got ahold of the book, read it, and loved it. Gary designed 2 oils: Oola Grow and Oola Balance, to pair with the book. Then in 2013, he created the Infused 7 kit, to make personal development and pulling the best out of you a multi-sensory experience. Oils work by hitting the limbic lobe of the brain when inhaled. That's

the emotional control center. They pair perfectly with the emotional side of finding balance in your life. This book will end with two scripts that train you how to use them with Oola.

Back to the OolaGuys ...

Dr. Troy Amdahl *(OolaGuru)* *and* Dr. Dave Braun *(OolaSeeker)* are currently traveling to all 50 states in a VW Surf Bus collecting 1,000,000 dreams and helping people find balance and growth in the 7 key areas of life *(the 7 F's of Oola)* – Fitness, Finance, Family, Field, Faith, Friends, and Fun. By

revealing how to remove the stress related to a life out of balance, they unlock the greatness that is inside all of us. A better *"you"* makes a better family, a better community, and ultimately a better world. The OolaGuys are committed to changing the world with their simple yet life-changing message.

Ready to dive in? The 7 F's are:

OOLAFitness: is health and wellness in your life, body, mind and soul. Eat less than you burn or burn more than you eat — that's the simple formula for good fitness. Your mind is the seat of all you do. Most choices are based on emotions, not physical responses. That's why Young Living's Infused 7 Oola oils collection is so incredible. It's an olfactory anchor for your nose.

OOLAFinance: is your personal finance — all income, spending, debt, charitable giving and saving and investing. What's the Oola rule? Spend less than you make.

OOLAFamily: is the scope of all your relationships. Harness pure love from healthy family relationships, identify toxic relationships and deal with them. Establish proper boundaries, offer forgiveness, or confront the issue.

OOLAField: is your career or your profession *(and that includes stay-at-home moms!)* What is the Oola mantra on field? Love it or leave it. If you're not crossing things off your bucket list in your field, or if you're operating in your comfort zone and never being stretched, it's time to evaluate if it's the best place for you to stay. Jon Acuff in his best-selling book *Quitter* said there's a difference between *"a day job and a dream job. Quit your day job to follow your dream, but only if you have a plan."* You'll spend one-third of your life at work. Make it something you love. Are you there to pay the bills, or do you GET to do your job?

OOLAFaith: is your belief system. It's your understanding of why you are here — your purpose, and what the Lord has created you for. Not sure what faith is all about? Get plugged in to a church near you. As you grow in your faith, you'll be more content and have a clearer purpose in this world.

OOLAFriends: is your social circle. Cut out toxic relationships. Surround yourself with people that inspire and challenge you. It's been said that you are a combination of your five closest friends. Who is in your space? Who do you give your ear? If the relationship is negative, passive-aggressive, gossip ridden or sarcastic, it may be time to take a step back. Fill your life with people who stretch you in good ways.

OOLAFun: is your personal passion in life. It's the things you enjoy doing in your downtime. Make sure you have a little fun every single day and that you have an active *"bucket list"* that's being checked off.

Take the free life balance test at: oolalife.com/step1

The 7 F's of Oola for Business:

Now we're going to kick this up a notch. What would the Oola Life look like if we put all seven of these areas under a business microscope? Can you truly have balance while growing a Young Living business? I believe you can, because I am living on the other side of that choice. It's not always pretty, but it's possible. Let's take a closer look at what business balance looks like.

OOLAFitness: is taking time every day to take care of your body, even if it's a 30-minute walk on a treadmill or a few squats and crunches before bed. That small time you invest in you will make you feel better, which will make your confidence increase, and lead to a stronger business. You may think these are not correlated, but they truly are. Before I sat down to write the next few pages of this book, I got a good run in. Yes, it cut into my writing time. But I know I feel better and write better when I take care of me. You may have spent a lot of time putting yourself at the bottom of the list, but that could be the entire root of the problem. If you never make the list, then you're going into every game depleted.

OOLAFinance: Hear my heart on this one closely. Do not spend more than you earn for your Young Living business. If you are faithful with the small things, the Lord will make you ruler over more! That means if your check is $ 80 a month with Young Living, you don't spend a penny over $ 80 a month. I like to challenge my leaders to forget that they have a check for the first six months and put it in their gas tank to teach classes. Go where the people are. As your team grows, you'll have more freedom to do generous recognition and fiery anonymous giving. In this stage, simply prove faithful with the small things and your platform will be increased. At every stage it goes back to self-control and discipline.

OOLAFamily: Your life should be in this order: God, spouse, family, work. That includes Young Living. If the balance is work first, your priorities are out of order. I'm not saying that if you're working an 8-hour day you need to play with your kids for 8 hours, too. I am saying that when the business needs to shut off, like at dinner, the cell phone is off and there is dedicated time daily to your kids and spouse. When this is in check, you will find your marriage does not go sour and you raise kids that respect your Young Living business. But it only works if your priorities are in the right place. If you are not respectful of them, they will not respect the work of your hands.

OOLAField: I believe 100 % that a Young Living business is the best job on earth. And to be honest, I never thought I'd hear those words leave my lips. You see, I love anchoring news. It's in my blood. I was created to write and speak. I still fill in a few times a month, because I love it. But it no longer owns me. Anchoring news 52 weeks a year at 4 a.m. kicked my life out of balance. My life is now back in balance.

> You decide what balance looks like for you.

How do I know Young Living is better than something I love??

You control it. You drive the car. You decide what balance looks like for you. And the perks to a Young Living business aren't too shabby, either.

· **The income is beyond our wildest dreams.**

Network marketing works. It's not a lottery, it's a mathematical certainty. The more you share, the more people fall in love, the larger your organization grows. The more develop passion for the lifestyle, the more get on Essential Rewards, the larger your base is each month. The larger your organization grows, the more people want to get their oils for free and develop into leaders duplicating your passion. It's a circle. We do better when we bless those beneath us. And the more you share, the more you grow. Two years out from retirement, my income is twelve times what I ever made anchoring news. I built it with one tool: a love of people.

The average Royal Crown Diamond makes $152,377 a month!?!? HELLO!! It's time to chase dreams! I consider Silver the first true game-changer income. (See Young Living Income Disclosure Statement on the following pages) It's more than I made monthly at my white-collar anchoring job of 22 years. Once you get there, you know you're going all the way. You know you have what it takes to build an organization, excite leaders, duplicate, and train the lifestyle. Make your first goal Silver. Run for freedom.

Other reasons to consider a Young Living business...

· **The timing has never been better.**

People are looking for chemical-free homes. They are reading labels. Large companies are changing their ingredients lists because you are asking for something better. That means you have 100 % market share. You can speak to men and women, kids and the elderly, those with means and those without — because you have what everyone wants: wellness.

· **You are your own boss and set your own hours.**

Waking up and dictating your own day is very Oola.

· **You can take time off and still get paid.**

How? In network marketing you amass a team. That team is still ordering and still teaching classes whether you are there or not. You're getting paid on that volume whether you show up to the ballgame or not. That means the business is there for you even when you can't always be there for the business. If I don't show up for a newscast, I lose my job. If I miss two weeks of work due to a family emergency, I go two weeks without a paycheck. That doesn't happen when you build a team with Young Living.

· **There is willable income.**

That means if something happens to you, and you have written a will, your Young Living income will go to whom you have willed it. This holds the power not only to change your financial future, but the financial legacy for those you love. Forever.

YOUNG LIVING 2016 U.S. INC[

As a direct selling company selling essential oils, supplements, and other lifestyle products, You
on our products.

Whatever your interest in the company, we hope to count you among the more than 2 million Y
home in the world.

What are my earning opportunities?

Members can earn commissions and bonuses as outlined in our Compensation Plan. As membe
opportunities.

This document provides statistical, fiscal data about the average member income and informati

RANK	PERCENTAGE OF ALL MEMBERS[3]	MONTHLY INC[	
		Lowest	Highest
Distributor	94.0%	$0	$841
Star	3.5%	$0	$811
Senior Star	1.3%	$1	$5,157
Executive	0.6%	$50	$12,139
Silver	0.2%	$562	$25,546
Gold	0.1%	$1,781	$46,820
Platinum	< 0.1%	$5,146	$85,993
Diamond	< 0.1%	$14,898	$140,333
Crown Diamond	< 0.1%	$37,227	$232,551
Royal Crown Diamond	< 0.1%	$58,392	$262,864

The income statistics in this statement are for incomes earned by all active U.S. members in 20'
the previous 12 months. The average annual income for all members in this time was $25, and t
did not make a purchase with Young Living in 2016. 57% of all members who enrolled in 2014 d

Note that the compensation paid to members summarized in this disclosure do not include exp
vary widely and might include advertising or promotional expenses, product samples, training,
members in this chart are not necessarily representative of the income, if any, that a Young Livin
not be considered as guarantees or projections of your actual earnings or profits. Your success
Living does not guarantee any income or rank success.

[1] Based on a count of all active members in 2016.
[2] Because a distributor's rank may change from during the year, these percentages are not based on individual distributor ranks throughout the
[3] Because a distributor's rank may change from during the year, these incomes are not based on individual distributor incomes throughout the e
[4] This is calculated by multiplying the average monthly incomes by 12.
[5] These statistics include all historical ranking data for each rank and thus is not limited to people who achieved these ranks in 2016.
[6] These incomes include income earned from January 1, 2016, and December 31, 2016, but which was paid between February 2016 and January
[7] Members who do not make at least one product purchase in the previous 12 months have their membership terminated.

]ME DISCLOSURE STATEMENT

ɹng Living offers opportunities for our members to build a business or simply receive discounts

Young Living members joining us in our mission to bring Young Living essential oils to every

ers move up in the ranks of Young Living, they become eligible for additional earning

ion about achieving various ranks.

OME[4]		ANNUALIZE AVERAGE INCOME[5]	MONTHS TO ACHIEVE THIS RANK[6]		
Median	*Average*		*Low*	*Average*	*High*
$0	$1	$12	N/A	N/A	N/A
$60	$77	$924	1	15	255
$197	$240	$2,880	1	22	255
$434	$514	$6,168	1	29	253
$1,783	$2,227	$26,724	1	36	251
$4,874	$6,067	$72,804	1	54	240
$12,188	$15,324	$183,888	2	63	238
$32,078	$39,566	$474,792	10	75	251
$64,256	$74,188	$890,256	14	83	236
$155,248	$152,377	$1,828,524	17	106	230

16. An "active" member is a member who made at least one product purchase in products in the median annual income for all members was $0. 51% of all members who enrolled in 2015 did not continue with Young Living in 2016.

ɔenses incurred by a member in the operation or promotion of his or her business, which can rent, travel, telephone and Internet costs, and miscellaneous expenses. The earnings of the ɪg member can or will earn through the Young Living Compensation Plan. These figures should will depend on individual diligence, work, effort, sales skill, and market conditions. Young

ː entire year, but based on the average distribution of distributor ranks during the entire year.
entire year, but based on earnings of all distributors qualifying for each rank during any month throughout the year.

y 2017.

· **Relationships.**

The people you meet along the way — your team, your upline, your crossline friends, will change your life for the better. They have the same vision you have: wellness, purpose, and abundance. They are swimming in the same direction. I cannot imagine my life now without the incredible friendships I've been blessed with.

· **Bonuses.**

I'm talking all-expenses-paid trips to the farms for Silver, Gold, Platinum and Diamond, separate phone lines for customer service, Facebook groups, and all kinds of swag at each rank. Young Living is a generous company.

· **Freedom.**

You can't free others when you are in bondage. I loved what I did, but I was chained. Freedom to me is giving generously. It's the ability to dictate your clock and your gifts. It's the chance to truly have balance because you control your life. You can't put a price tag on freedom.

Let's jump back into the other Oola F's and peek at them from the angle of business.

OOLAFaith: if you have a Christ-centered business, and all your decisions are made from that perspective, you'll be honored in the marketplace, because your goal is always that the Lord gets the glory for your work. It's not about you, it's about Him. It's about servant-led leadership. Biblical values. Integrity when no one is looking. Gratitude for what's been given and what's been earned. Always putting the distributor above yourself, and seeing their needs met first. When you come from that vantage point with your business, from a place of faith, there is honor in your workspace and duplication of gratitude and integrity in your leaders. What do you do when no one is looking? Do you run your business with integrity? If it comes from a place of faith, the entire core of your decision-making process is on solid ground. Always look at your actions through this lens.

OOLAFriends: This is where Young Living truly comes into play. I did not realize as a working mom how isolated I was! I got up, sat in a room for eight hours and talked to a wall, came home and homeschooled all day, played mom taxi, made dinner and collapsed. It was the same routine for 22 years. The thrill of the newsroom was fun, but I'd be lying if I said I had a slew of deep friendships. I had a few friends I texted regularly and called on the phone —and I had a few that I visited with a couple of times a month. I could count my deep friendships on a few fingers. Young Living has completely changed this for me. I can truly say I have friends in all 50 states that have my back. If something were to happen, I know there would be heavy prayer coverage, friends at my door, and financial and emotional support. It's because Young Living is a family. There is deep concern and compassion within its members. When one is hurt, the others flock. I've seen it on my own team, I've seen it with teams of people I've never met, I've seen it among the Diamonds — selfless giving. It's a theme from the newest distributor to the Royal Crown Diamonds. It's because we all seek a common purpose, and we strive toward it with positive vision and focus. Simply watch the end of the month rank ups on all the teams — leaders hopping on crossline leader's pages to rally them on and support them, words of encouragement, notes and flowers in the mail. I have seen Royal Crown Diamonds whispering encouragement into the ears of Senior Stars in convention hallways. It doesn't matter who you are or what your rank is. You have value in this company. The friendships you will forge as you labor side by side in the trenches and build a legacy for your family — those friendships will last for life.

SURROUND YOURSELF
▬ WITH ▬
PEOPLE THAT
Inspire You

OOLAFun: In the past 12 months, I've had the ability to set my feet in Hawaii, Singapore, Malaysia, Indonesia, Mexico, and Banff, Canada — because of this company. I LOVE traveling. So for me, that's fun. *(You can also build an entire Diamondship from your couch and never* *leave your home, if that's your heart's desire).* I also love gardening. And running. And scuba diving. And reading to my kids. And dating my husband of 20 years. I have so much more time on my clock since I dropped my 40-hour-a-week job that I'm truly able to enjoy those things at a new level. You have to get a little fun in your day every single day, even if it's a month that you're hustling for a rank. It may be connecting with someone who inspires you — praying with a prayer warrior for a few moments, snuggling with one of your littles or taking a twenty-minute bath with a little Stress Away to decompress. Make a list of the things that bring you joy, and don't work yourself to the end of every day. That leads to bitterness, which will foster bitterness for your business. It also can put your spouse in a place where they foster bitterness for your business. It just requires balance. For fun to get in the mix, you have to add it to the list deliberately. It never shows up there on its own. This is the trickiest, because we tend to leave it off. But you'll find contentment with your business when you give yourself the freedom to play. What is your *"play"* list? Get it on paper and get it done. It's as important as your hustle list. You'll stick to this a lot longer if you build in joy.

We've run through Oola in the Oola style, and Oola from the Gameplan business vantage point. Now I want you to do an honest self-evaluation. This is as Oola as it gets: do a good gut check, a vulnerable and honest assessment of where you are in this moment, then take action steps to dig out. If you're not doing a good check three or four times a year, you need to. Be completely honest as you fill the next few pages out. This is just between you and you. If you're honest, it will show you which parts of your life are way out of line. Then I'll spend the second half of the book training you how to rein them back in and give you practical time management tips geared toward a Young Living business.

The OolaWheel: Know Your Weaknesses

Rate each of the areas of your life from 1-10, with 10 being the best/ most true. Then divide your score by 10 in each area. Mark it on the OolaWheel, with the lowest numbers being closest to the center. Here's a sample of a finished OolaWheel. Your *"valve"* is the area of your life most out of whack.

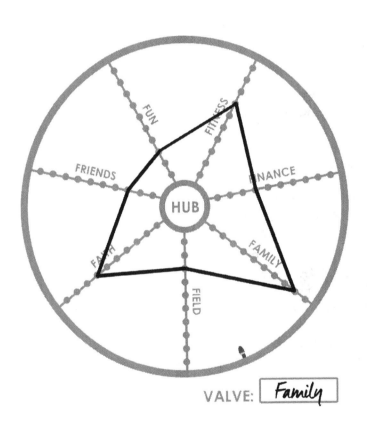

VALVE: *Family*

OolaFitness

1) I would rate my current health * _____
2) How close am I to my ideal weight? * _____
3) I would rate my overall mental health * _____
4) I do at least 3 cardio/resistance sessions per week * * * * * * * * * * * * _____
5) How hard do I push myself during exercise? * * * * * * * * * * * * * * * * _____
6) I actively exercise outside * _____
7) I practice relaxation daily * _____
8) I love my life and have little stress * _____
9) My meals are nutrient rich and the proper calories for my body * _____
10) I eat a balanced diet and avoid processed and fast food * * * * * * * _____

Total score _____ /10 = _____

OolaFinance

1) I would rate my personal finances * _____
2) I am saving at least 10 % of every dollar I make * * * * * * * * * * * * * * _____
3) I am completely debt free *(minus my mortgage)* * * * * * * * * * * * * _____
4) My monthly income exceeds my monthly expenses * * * * * * * * * * * _____
5) I am investing at least 15 % for retirement * * * * * * * * * * * * * * * * * * _____
6) I have an emergency account equaling at least 7 months of expenses _____
7) I have the proper insurance *(health, life, property, etc...)* * * * * _____
8) I give my money generously and without expectationions * * * * * _____
9) I have a complete and updated will * _____
10) I have a solid budget and stick to it every month * * * * * * * * * * * _____

Total score _____ /10 = _____

OolaFamily

1) I would rate my current family situation * * * * * * * * * * * * * * * * * _____
2) We eat at least one meal per day together as a family * * * * * * * * * _____
3) My immediate and extended family is functional * * * * * * * * * * * * _____
4) Thinking of family makes me feel happy * * * * * * * * * * * * * * * * * _____
5) I am honest with my family members * * * * * * * * * * * * * * * * * * * _____
6) I work hard at being a better family member * * * * * * * * * * * * * * * _____
7) I set aside personal time with my family without phones * * * * * * _____
8) My family is loving, patient, supportive, and respectful * * * * * * * * _____
9) I hold no hurt feelings toward any family members * * * * * * * * * * _____
10) I feel as though I spend enough time with my family to meet their needs _

Total score _____ /10 = _____

OolaField

1) I would rate my overall job satisfaction * * * * * * * * * * * * * * * * * * _____
2) My job financially meets my needs * _____
3) I love my job * _____
4) I feel as if I am doing what I was created to do * * * * * * * * * * * * * _____
5) I have solid goals for my field * _____
6) My current job doesn't interfere with my family and personal time_____
7) My current job makes the world a better place * * * * * * * * * * * * * _____
8) My job utilizes my natural gifts and abilities * * * * * * * * * * * * * * * _____
9) My current job can support my long-term financial goals * * * * * * _____
10) My job offers the opportunity to grow * * * * * * * * * * * * * * * * * * _____

Total score _____ /10 = _____

OolaFaith

1) I would rate my faith * _____

2) I feel connected to a higher purpose * _____

3) I am plugged into a faith community to continue to learn or grow _____

4) I spend at least 20 minutes a day in prayer and meditation * * * * * _____

5) My beliefs and the way I live my life are congruent * * * * * * * * * * * _____

6) I use my faith to help resolve conflict and issues in my life * * * * * _____

7) I reflect on my faith throughout the day * * * * * * * * * * * * * * * * * * _____

8) I forgive easily * _____

9) I rely on my faith to guide my choices and decisions * * * * * * * * * _____

10) I feel comfortable sharing and teaching my faith to others * * * * _____

Total score _____ /10 = _____

OolaFriends

1) I would rate my social network of friends * * * * * * * * * * * * * * * * _____

2) I have unconditionally loving, supportive, and empowering friends _____

3) I am satisfied with the number of friendships in my life * * * * * * * _____

4) I am a good example/mentor for my friends * * * * * * * * * * * * * * _____

5) My friends support my dreams and are good examples or mentors _____

6) When I think of my three closest friends, I have no stress * * * * * _____

7) I openly communicate and trust my friends * * * * * * * * * * * * * * * * _____

8) I have friends who are good mentors in all 7 F's of Oola * * * * * * * _____

9) I have no hard feelings or ill will toward my present friendships * _____

10) I am not judgmental toward my friends * * * * * * * * * * * * * * * * * * _____

Total score _____ /10 = _____

Oola Fun

1) I would rate fun in my life * _____

2) I enjoy and am having fun in life * _____

3) I try new things often * _____

4) I have fun and invest time pursuing my personal passion * * * * * * _____

5) I have fun outside work at least 3 times per week * * * * * * * * * * * * * _____

6) I check off at least one *"Bucket List"* item each year * * * * * * * * * _____

7) I am a fun person to be around * _____

8) Fun rarely interferes with my responsibilities * * * * * * * * * * * * * * _____

9) People would say I am a fun person * _____

10) I easily find free fun in simple everyday life * * * * * * * * * * * * * * _____

Total score _____ /10 = _____

What are your top five bucket list items? List them below and start to cross them off!

1) _____

2) _____

3) _____

4) _____

5) _____

Now let's complete your OolaWheel. Identify where you are most out of balance. It will cue you where to start. If you don't want to fill the OolaWheel out on paper, head to oolalife.com/step1 and do it online for free.

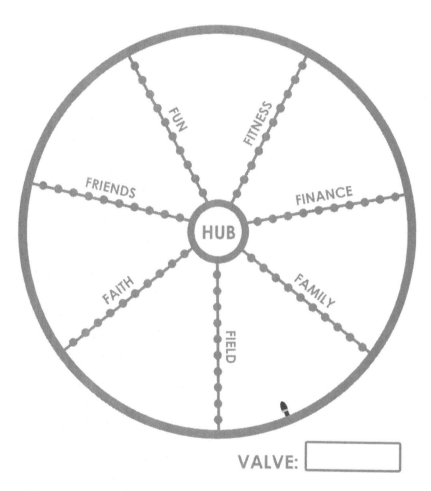

VALVE: [　　　　　　　　]

(Total each area and divide by 10. Put a dot on the OolaWheel for each "F". The closer it is to the center, the more in balance that area of your life is. Look at your "spokes" at the end to see which parts of your life need the most attention.)

You are probably looking at the OolaWheel and saying *"hey, wait a second! I picked up an Oola for business book already feeling completely overwhelmed with my Young Living business, and now I'm not only overwhelmed with business, but also with the six other areas of my life!"* I am here to tell you that's completely normal!

Your goal is Royal Crown Diamond, right? I have never met a Royal Crown Diamond, Crown Diamond, or Diamond that said they were perfectly at peace with every area of their life, and their business was built in a state of complete focus with no distraction, frustration at the juggle, irritation, stalling at certain ranks, and flawless balance. One hundred percent of the leaders I have interviewed told me it was a day to day trial to master business and life simultaneously. Some days they did better than other days. And yet they still made it to the top. The ones that make it aren't the ones that are flawless. They are the ones that don't quit. They are the ones that do a little every single day. Daily investments lead to a big yield. So let's teach you balance and consistency, not how to be perfect. It's about changing your goals. A goal of perfect balance is unattainable. A goal of consistency and daily investments is VERY attainable. And it will get you to Diamond. Let me make a case for the change of language.

> A goal of consistency and daily investments is VERY attainable.

With your *"regular"* 9 to 5 job, do you feel like you have life in perfect balance? Always stack your Young Living business against what you are doing right now. I can tell you most days as a news anchor I felt battle weary, adrenally done, and a master of nothing. If you can't nail the juggle with what you are doing now, why put that pressure on yourself with your Young Living business? That is a very high expectation.

Why You Need To Be Deliberate About Balance

I did a little digging online to see how much we're actually doing at the office. Research suggests that in an eight-hour day, the average worker is only productive for two hours and 53 minutes. That's right--you're only productive for around 3 hours a day. According to the Bureau of Labor Statistics, the average American works 8.8 hours every day. A vouchercloud.com study of nearly 2,000 full-time office workers revealed that most people aren't working most of the time they're at work.

The most popular unproductive activities listed were:

1) Reading websites - 1 hour, 5 minutes
2) Checking social media - -44 minutes
3) Discussing non-work-related things with co-workers - 40 minutes
4) Searching for new jobs - 26 minutes
5) Taking smoke breaks - 23 minutes
6) Making calls to partners or friends - 18 minutes
7) Making hot drinks - 17 minutes
8) Texting or instant messaging - 14 minutes
9) Eating snacks - 8 minutes
10) Making food in office - 7 minutes

One of the blessings of network marketing is that is doesn't take 40 hours a week to become a seven-figure earner. The little droplets you invest will be enough to build the castle brick by brick into something so much larger than you ever dreamed. You CAN do this side by side with your life. You CAN fit it in, even if the task seems insurmountable. You just have to make the decision to do it daily, and with purpose and intent in how you spend your minutes. When every second is precious, every second has to count. Go into your Young Living work hours with deliberation. If you're putting three hours into your Young Living work day, you have just been more productive than at a 40 hour a week job. *(That's at 40 hours a week — a full-time pace. I have never worked at that rate, and I hit Diamond two and a half years after getting my starter kit.)* From the beginning, I have worked my Young Living business no more than 10 hours a week. I teach one two-hour class a week, I spend about six hours building relationships to get people to come to classes and marketing my classes, and the rest is spent in follow up and training leaders. Based on the ratio of productive time versus the work week, I'd need to work just 43 minutes a day to equal the same productivity as a 40 hour a week job. And this job can make me a millionaire.

There is one more thing I want to hit on before we do some training on how to spin the plates you have in the air. That's mindset. There are things that will pull you far away from your goals, and things that will accelerate you toward them. In Oola terms, they are called OolaBlockers and OolaAccelerators. Let's talk about them in a business setting for just a moment.

"Time Management is really a misnomer — the challenge is not to manage time, but to manage ourselves."

— Stephen R. Covey

OolaBlockers

Fear

Unrealistic fear can paralyze you and prevent you from taking actions that will move you forward. A complete disregard of fear can expose you to risks that can take you down. (Oola, p 102).

Of all of the OolaBlockers, I think this is the most dangerous. One of the biggest business mistakes that I see is an unwillingness to share oils with people — and it's all rooted in fear. Fear of what they will think of you, fear of being rejected with a big *"no"*, fear of not getting results, fear of not ranking, fear of their thoughts on network marketing, fear of losing friendships, fear that they will think they are getting swindled into paying more for a product. It all goes back to fear. Here's my Fear tip: love them SO much that you see past your fear. The wellness of their family matters more than your fear. Speak to them.

Guilt

We all make mistakes, and we all have said and done things that make us feel guilty. Persistent guilt becomes a real OolaBlocker that can really hinder you from the life you want. Experiencing guilt is not a crime. Choosing to carry guilt with you every day is. (Oola, p 108).

Where does guilt come from in a Young Living business? Not every leader will like your leadership style. Not every distributor or potential distributor will like the way you teach. Relationships may go sour. Some may take a different path or choose to run their business in a way you don't agree with. Many times, we wish we could go back and change our words. You may get frustrated with a family member or spouse that, despite your best efforts, cannot seem to understand a lifestyle of wellness — and it comes to a head over and over again in your conversations. Guilt can come from many places. My tip: ask for forgiveness and let it go. If it's a leader that has their own plans and is swimming upstream in a downstream team, let them lead their business the way they choose, and honor their choices. If it's a family member that sees no purpose in oils, love on them as if oils never existed in your conversations, without any strings attached. Release is my favorite oil for these types of situations. You can never change how people respond to you. But you can change how you respond to them. If there are words you regret since you have started your business, connect with the person and apologize, and treat them with dignity and respect, no matter what they believe.

Anger

Being persistently or violently angry affects not only you, but everyone around you, and can bring consequences that you will live with forever. If you harbor anger and let it slowly eat away at your soul, it will des your chances for an Oola life. (Oola, p 114).

This may not be an area that you deeply struggle with — so let me tweak the words a bit to show you how this may apply to you. Frustration leads to anger. Letting small things get to you is a form of anger. Is your reaction stronger than it needs to be? Is your response proportional to the situation? In business terms, do you get irritated when your kids interrupt your work time? Does your home suffer while you are focusing? Does your spouse suffer while you are working? When classes don't turn out as planned, or if there are no-shows, do you carry that frustration back through your front door and spew it on members of your family? How you respond is everything. Lead a grace-centered business. Emotionally detach yourself from the sale of the starter kit. Anger is a major OolaBlocker.

Self-Sabotage

Subconscious negative self-talk speaks up, you decide that you are not worth it, and you unknowingly begin the process of self-sabotage. (Oola, p 120).

Why? Don't let the enemy mess with your head like that. Listen to the words out of your mouth for the next 24 hours. Better yet, listen to the unspoken words in your head. Are you blessing or cursing your business with your own tongue? There is nothing in between! Speak LIFE. Your thoughts and words have such tremendous power. We have a saying on the Oil Ability team: tongue, head, feet. Say your dreams out loud, even if you do not believe them yet. Your head will start to follow. And your feet will follow after that. It works! Say your dreams so many times out loud there is not an inch where they can't happen.

Is there a part of you that truly doesn't see a Royal Crown Diamond paycheck in your future? Is there a part of you that doesn't feel like you have earned it? Is there a part of you that thinks you don't have what it takes to go all the way? Is there a part of you that thinks you are not worth it? Is there a part of you that's had your dreams and hopes crushed so many times that you are afraid to dream again?

Stop.

Open scripture.

"For I know the plans I have for you, says the Lord. Plans to prosper you. Plans for a hope and a future."

— Jeremiah 29:11

It doesn't say plans to keep you in poverty. Plans for a hard life. Plans with no dreams. Plans with no vision. Plans for stress. Plans for exhaustion. Plans for desertion. Plans to be abandoned. Plans to have your hopes dashed. Plans to have freedom stolen. It says plans to prosper. Prosperity is written in your future, if you will fight. The Lord will not hand it to you. It takes rolling up your sleeves and hard work — and allowing yourself to dream when you feel like you have no dreams yet, and when you feel you have no dreams left. You see, money in the hands of good people can go so very far. There are people that have yet to join your team who need the wellness, purpose and abundance that Young Living has to offer — if only you will speak up. If only you will fight for them. If only you believe in yourself enough to be bold. Don't build your business to the point that you plateau and stop doing the things that grew it in the first place — simply because you can't see yourself at the next rank. You won't get there unless you can see the paycheck, see the freedom, and speak it over yourself every single day until it happens. Freedom for you means freedom for thousands who will join your team. Write out your goals. Write out your dreams. Write out your fears and write the opposite of them. And then speak hope and life over yourself, no matter how inadequate you may feel. God has a funny way of using little people to do big things.

Laziness

Anyone at the top of their game has one thing in common — they are not lazy. They are passionate about their life and worked very hard to get to the top. On the path to Oola, there is no room for lazy. It cannot be part of your life in any way, shape, or form. Lazy blocks Oola. What the lazy want, the disciplined get. (Oola, p 126).

This business takes hard work. If anyone tells you otherwise, they are lying to you. It is not easy. It takes getting past fear, speaking with people you do not know, building relationships, picking up a phone and checking in with people, dealing with dissident and absent leaders, fighting distraction and exhaustion and disappointment when things don't happen on your timeline. It takes brushing off the noes and still standing at the end of the week. You cannot take things personally; you must see the good in people even when you feel let down. It takes kicking the dust off your feet. Not sweating the small stuff. Staying so busy teaching classes you don't have time for disappointment or analyzing why your friend didn't show up for class. You must learn new skills like marketing and the art of listening. Learning how to share your story. Fighting off the doubt and negative self-talk in your own head. You will be your biggest obstacle as you build! There are a lot of pieces in a Young Living business! But one thing that cannot exist is laziness.

This business will not come fast and it will not come easy. It's built one brick at a time, one relationship at a time. It's built one class at a time. It's not built with one Rockstar, and it's not built with a handful of large orders or a great Young Living promotion. It's built with a thousand yeses. It's built with a hundred classes. It's built with ten thousand dreams. And it's built by picking yourself up and continuing to walk. The only people who don't make it to Diamond are the ones that stop walking.

Now that I've painted a frightening picture for you of how this all goes down, pause and walk with me on the other side. What if you overcome this Oola Blocker? What does freedom feel like? Waking up every day and not owing a penny to anyone. Looking out the window and owning your clock. You can spend your seconds and your hours EXACTLY how you choose. Seeing a need and giving anonymously without it affecting the dinner on your kitchen table that night. Seeing dreams you have had for 20, 30, or 40 years realized. Taking care of family. Taking care of you. Diamond retreats with some of the most amazing people you've ever met... for the rest of your life. Having a front row seat to watch hundreds and hundreds of your leaders rank and experience the same freedom in their lives. Is it easy? No. Is it worth it? Yes. That is what waits for you on the other side. It's relational freedom. Spiritual freedom. Financial freedom. Mental freedom. Physical freedom. Time freedom. Freedom in every imaginable way. Your chains are gone.

THE REAL
METHOD
TO MY MADNESS
WAS
Consistency

But you only get there with discipline. By constantly teaching — by sharing oils, in whatever way that looks like for you — whatever way gets results. If there is only one skill that you master from this entire little book, it must be the art of sharing. The art of getting oils on people and leading them to a starter kit. There are no leaders and there is no Essential Rewards base if you're not out there sharing your love of oils. It all hinges on the art of sharing. And sharing is hard work. If you are teaching one class a month, it will take a very long time for you to rank. That's hobby level. Stop treating your business as a hobby and start treating it like a career that leads to freedom. No one will build your freedom for you — that falls on your shoulders. But you must move from the place you are and commit to sharing regularly, or you'll still be in the pit ten years from now. By regularly, I mean a class a week. Nothing gets you out of exhaustion like fighting. There is no replacement for hard work. All you need to do this is a 3-page script and a starter kit, no bells and whistles. That script is in the *Gameplan* book, and thousands have ranked with it. The more bells and whistles that you have above and beyond the script, the harder it is for your leaders to duplicate. Always ask yourself if what you are doing can be copied. If the answer is no, stop it. Throw in some fight and a lot of consistency and you have the recipe for a flawless Diamondship.

Envy

Envy is worse than jealousy. Jealousy is wanting what others have. Envy is wanting what others have and wanting them not to have it. Envy can suck the joy out of life. (Oola, p 132).

I believe at some point, all of us have looked over our shoulder. All of us have seen a Diamond rank in record time, had someone on our team either surpass our current rank or rank faster in the early ranks than we ever did. Or grow side by side with a crossline friend only to plateau and see them achieve things you have had on your heart for many months or years, while you sit stagnant. Here's my words for envy: don't compare yourself to ANYONE but you. If you look at your OGV, your organizational group volume, and it's higher this month than it was 12 months ago, you are doing something right. If it's not as high as you want it to be, focus on the three things that grow your business: teach classes, get people on essential rewards, and train your leaders. Don't make excuses and don't compare. Do the things that grow your volume and create duplication on your team. Focus on your organization, your time, your sharing, your love of people — and you'll be so busy growing you that you won't have time to dwell on what others have built.

Focus

If you lack focus, you cannot endure what it takes to balance and grow. Focus becomes an OolaBlocker if it takes one of two forms: lack of focus, or misdirected focus. Delayed gratification is very Oola. Focusing on the larger goal will give you the strength you need to sacrifice now to win later. (Oola, p 140).

Always ask yourself if what you are doing will lead to growth on your team. When you have those short moments to pour into your business, they have to be deliberate — especially if you are in a season of life where you are pressed for time. I have had the honor of speaking with thousands of business builders over the last year in 31 different cities on the Gameplan book tour. It's given me a unique perspective to hear your hearts and your struggles. And one of the most common questions I hear is *"I just don't see how it can be done. I don't see how you can grow your business and care for your family at the same time."*

When I investigate the organizations of those struggling with time management, there's a common theme. They either are not working the business at all there is no consistency to their sharing, or they are working the business a LOT but not doing any income-producing activities. They are treading water.

What does that look like? Spending three hours on a coaching call with one of your strong leaders when you need to be coaching the new business builders on your weak legs. Making a big spread of food made with vitality oils for a 101 class — something your leaders can't afford to duplicate. Planning and running large events instead of teaching classes. Scrolling Facebook for hours. Going for aromatherapy certifications. Doing make and take classes with fifteen different supplies on websites that are not the Young Living Virtual Office. Making things pretty for a class with folders and hand outs and colored posterboard *(not duplicable)*.

When I look out at the sea of things that I did to go Diamond, there's truly only one thing that stands out: I taught 288 101 classes. My six aromatherapy certifications did not build my OGV. They were a mistake that would have shaved a year off my time to rank. All the make and takes I put together — no one re-ordered the oils or made the projects again. The specialty classes I taught on animals and emotions that did not drive to one of the four starter kits — oils, Savvy, Thieves or NingXia — did not lead to wholesale accounts. They did not reorder in the Virtual Office. What's the one thing that got results? What is the one thing that catapulted me to Diamond? It wasn't the books I read or the number of plant species I memorized for my aromatherapy exams. It was the number of people I talked to about Young Living oils. If you are going to fulfill Gary Young's mission of getting oils into every home in the world, you have to spend 80% of your time sharing. Have you plateaued? You have to continue to spend more than three quarters of your time sharing even if you are a Silver, Gold, Platinum or Diamond leader. Legs and OGV don't build themselves — it takes tenacity and FOCUS. If you stop teaching and start playing the role of the leader, your team stops teaching, too. They will do what they see you doing. Stay humble and stay in the trenches. Do what grows your team.

How are you spending your time? Are you treading water, or swimming for land? If your time is tight, you can't afford to make mistakes. You'll put yourself in a place where you begin to believe that network marketing doesn't work. But there are 450 Diamonds in Young Living! It works! If you want to be one of them, you need to focus. You need to do things that lead to growth. You need to do things that your leaders can copy. You need to stop scaring your leaders off with your knowledge, by being the expert, or by making things pretty. Use third party tools like Your Gameplan *(the mini)* for prospecting, the Gameplan series for leader training, Oola: Find Balance in an Unbalanced World, Oola for Women, or many of the other amazing Young Living tools out there. Point to resources and don't be all things to all people. Don't lose your time on activities that don't yield OGV, ER, or excite your leaders. You'll get burnt out and you'll plateau. The secret to success is constant focus. If you take your eye off the ball, you lose precious time. If you lose time, you lose momentum.

Point to resources and don't be all things to all people.

Don't get sidetracked.

That covers all the OolaBlockers. Now we're going to switch gears for a moment and focus on encouragement. There are things that will turbocharge your path to Diamond. They are called OolaAccelerators, and they are just that: they are Nitro for your business. Include these attributes and showcase leaders who do them well on your business pages, and you'll generate a spirit of humility and gratitude among the leaders of your team.

OolaAccelerators

Gratitude

Be grateful for and love where you are, where you want to go, and where you have been. Be grateful for every part of the journey. Consider the really bad stuff — is it possible to be grateful for losing your job, getting in an accident, or having a sick child? The hidden gifts from these so-called bad things can take months, years, or a lifetime to be revealed. The faster you see the purpose and become truly grateful for the experience, the more the door opens. (Oola, p 150).

When you come to a fork in the road, you have two options: let it eat you alive, or find the tidbit of good in the situation, focus on that, and keep moving. If you dwell in the land of the negative, it is hard to grow a Young Living business, because people will only follow what they want. They won't follow negativity. Gratitude is the opposite of negativity. If you emulate it on your business and product pages, in what you post on social media, and live it with your speech and the way you act, you'll start to see your leaders emulating gratitude also. A team that is thankful is a team that bonds. A team that bonds is a team that edifies one another. And that's something people want to be around — it leads to more and more growth, organically. Even when you are in your lowest places, find the one beam of sunlight. Gratitude leads me out when I am in desperation. At every stage of your business and at every rank, never lose sight of the blessing that you have in Young Living. You have been given a precious gift. Share it with the world.

Love

Love is the lightening bolt of all OolaAccelerators. It is so powerful! To give and receive love produces passion. (Oola, p 160).

You need two gifts to do this business well: passion and compassion. Passion for the products Young Living makes — a deep love for getting all the yuck out of your home, for protecting the four walls of your house and training others to do the same. Then you need compassion for where people are. You need to meet them in that place without judgement, even if there's not a wink of their life that oozes clean living. You do that with love. You season your words with grace. It comes from caring about the people in front of you. That's the meaning of it all, right? That's why we share. It's why we put ourselves out there. It's why we do hard things. It's why we step outside our comfort zone. If I had to pick one *"why"* for a Young Living business — to sum the whole thing up in one word, it would be love. If you start from that place, everything else seems to fade away — fear, envy, self-sabotage, anger... nothing else matters when you're in it to serve. Then it's always about them, no matter what angle you take your business from. If you can keep it about the distributor, the work of your hands will always be multiplied. Care more about them than what it can do for you, in every circumstance.

Discipline

Rarely will you find someone who has succeeded in attaining the life of their dreams without a strong work ethic and discipline. Oola is not for the undisciplined. (Oola, p 168).

I am convinced that this is the central theme of this entire mini book. It doesn't matter what your hustle looks like if your hustle is sporadic. It doesn't matter what your passion looks like if your leaders only see it once a month. It doesn't matter how amazing your classes are if you rarely teach. It doesn't matter how much you love your distributors if you never touch base with them on essential rewards. Discipline is the rhythm that your Young Living business must march to for you to succeed. If you can get a cadence down — a pattern to when you do certain things each month with intent, your likelihood of ranking goes up exponentially.

What do I mean with all this talk!?

I end my month by setting up 4-6 classes for the next month. I start marketing. While I am waiting for the window to teach, I do all my follow up in one sitting. I have clipboards with names and contacts of every person that came to a class. Then I hustle and spend 80 % of my time building relationships, marketing, or teaching classes. Rinse and repeat — over and over and over again. The last week I am always setting up classes, then doing follow up as I market, then teaching my tush off. Find your rhythm.

Repeat until you have a Diamondship. All successful Young Living businesses are built on the back of discipline. Self-control is a fruit of the Spirit! It might mean forgoing a little bit of pleasure in the short term. But the payout for the long term far surpasses the smidge of pleasure you have missed along the journey.

Integrity

Be wary of stepping over the line, especially the gray line, to speed up the process of ranking. It happens to the best of us. We want it so badly. We use justification to act in a way that is out of integrity to get us to our goals faster. This will catch up with you, and it will end badly. (Oola, p 178).

I mentioned it earlier... what do you do when no one is watching? Let me dig a bit deeper. What do you do when you have chances to work, but you intentionally choose to rest? You hit the snooze button a few more times. You could make a call to a leader or to someone who came to class, because the house is silent — but you scroll Facebook instead. You have been sitting at Executive rank for two years with your legs and OGV in place, and only 8 kits missing from your PGV — but you don't teach the two classes you need to teach to get the rank. You sit just outside it, saying you can't get anyone to come to class. But your check would spike by $1,500 a month if you just hunkered down and taught. To me, that's an integrity issue. The Lord has trusted you with something precious, and every month, you toss that $1,500 blessing into a fire pit, unclaimed by your lack of work.

Justification is a slippery slope. Do not justify laziness and say you don't have time to build. Do not skip the opportunity to look for fat in your clock — so you can squeeze one hour in for your Young Living business. Do not do things that are morally wrong because no one will see. Read through the Policies and Procedures document under *"Member Resources"* in the Virtual Office and make sure you are setting the trend on your team to follow the rules.

I believe with my whole heart that honesty will be returned to you. It will find its way back in your lowest moments. Justification is a thorn that tears your business down act by act. Choose to do the right things, because that's what will be duplicated under you. A leader with integrity is a precious jewel on your team. Be that leader.

Passion

If life were a card game, passion is the trump card. If your passion is strong enough, it has the ability to trump many of the OolaBlockers, like fear, anger, and laziness. Tapping into your passion will empower you to overcome. (Oola, p 186).

Get really good at sharing your story. Facts tell, stories sell. Start every class with how you got involved with oils and why you love them — why you can't live without them. Share with enthusiasm, as if it's the first moment you saw an oil work! Always begin from that place of rawness and realness, no matter how long you do this. That is the spark that will lead to the kit. Your personal recommendation and your love of oils is what gets people to try them. If you always begin from that place, you will have their attention immediately. Sit down and take some time to write out your story. It may be only 30 seconds long, and that's completely ok! If you can passionately share your why, you will help others find theirs.

Humility

It's quiet confidence. Park your ego at the door. You can learn the importance of humility two ways: 1) by practicing it, or 2) the hard way... by living it. Ever heard of pride before the fall? Learn humility or be humbled. Your choice. (Oola, p 194).

Does ego come naturally for you? Do you find yourself talking about... yourself? Does your mind wander to your own accomplishments? Do you feed off the positive things people say about you? If you're in that place, hear my heart. No one will follow that forever.

The most powerful tool you have in your business is the gift of duplication, leaders that copy things that lead to growth. If you are scaring your leaders away with a lack of humility, you lose duplication. Until you can train your tongue in meekness, train it to do one other thing: edification.

What do I mean by that? Every time you wish to boast, instead take it as an opportunity to show off one of the leaders in your downline. Grab a Facebook photo of them and share one of their talents. Share how they inspired you. Share something they are good at. Share a post they did that was wildly successful. Brag on their way of teaching or leading or follow up. Love on them. A lot. Edify them in front of their leaders. Edify them in front of their spouses. Edify them in front of other crossline leaders. Edify them when they are there and when they will never see what you are doing. I think the fastest way to untrain yourself from focusing on you is to focus on those around you.

The best part is when your team picks up on it, and they start edifying their leaders, too. It creates an entire culture of praise. And THAT is something people will follow.

Wisdom

Wisdom is more than just knowledge. There are a lot of very smart people who are not wise. Wisdom is unique because it leans heavily on logic, and little on emotion. You can become wise at a young age if you are open to learning from the experiences of others. (Oola, p 202).

The key to all wisdom was nestled in the sentence just above this one: learn from the experiences of others. Train your brain. You may start with a little Jim Rohn on Youtube, or head to an Eric Worre *"Go Pro"* conference, or the

> When you get to the place where you feel you have nothing to learn, you have lost something precious.

Young Living International Grand convention, or pick up some incredible books by Dale Carnegie on Amazon. The moment you stop learning is the instant you stop growing. I will never know all there is to know about network marketing. Not even when I have been a Royal Crown Diamond for 50 years. I change, the industry changes, the marketplace changes. My relentless pursuit of wisdom remains constant.

There is always something to learn from those around you, above you, below you, and in the room with you. I learn from my kids every single day! One of the things that will truly catapult you in this business is having a teachable spirit. Be willing to admit when you have made a mistake, even if it's publicly. Let your leaders see you attend events and train your brain in those quiet moments with a podcast in your car. Always be willing to let go of the *"way you do things."* Stay coachable. I promise you, you'll rank so much faster if you stay in a place where you don't know it all.

I have had the honor of getting to know just about every Royal Crown Diamond in Young Living personally. Do you know one attribute that I see in every single one of them? They are humble. They are eager to learn. There is not one of them that I don't deeply respect. I just got back from my first Diamond retreat, and I took a leader with me who had only been in the business for 10 weeks. In those ten weeks, she had gone Executive and Silver in the same month, doubled her OGV the second month, and added another Silver in one under her. She had a goal of Diamond in eight months.

No matter who we were sitting next to, every Diamond asked for her story. Every Diamond asked her system, and what she did to rank. Every Diamond wanted to hear about her way of sharing. Here was a woman who'd been in the business for 10 weeks, training multi-millionaires! It was a neat thing to see, but I think my favorite part of the story was that the Diamonds were open to ideas. And that's exactly why they are Diamonds.

When you get to the place where you feel you have nothing to learn, you have lost something precious. Always listen to the stories around you. Always soak in the knowledge and gifts and talents of others. Always look for ways to improve your game. And always be willing to tweak your methods, especially if you are in a rut. Don't be so busy learning that you're not out there teaching classes! But at the same time, never shut off your ears. Set the example on your team of being coachable, no matter what your title is. Sit with the newest leader and give them your time. Get lost in the stories on your team. Let other leaders in your downline teach on your business page. Iron sharpens iron.

Tools to Get Your Feet Moving

n one little mini book, we have now hit on the entire heart of Oola. I've taken you through the 7 F's, the *OolaWheel, OolaBlockers and Oola Accelerators*. The rest of this book will be filled with specific tools and tactics to help you balance your business. Will you still have days where you feel overwhelmed after applying some of these things? Absolutely. But there is a lot of wisdom in the next few pages, gathered from thousands of posts on the Oil Ability with Sarah Facebook page, interviews with Diamonds and up, wisdom from the Oola guys, from me and more — that will give you solid direc-

tion as you try every day to keep all those plates in your life spinning. Start with the plate that your Oola wheel showed was most lacking and move from there. We are going to perfectly meld Gameplan and Oola together as one by giving you 40 top time management tips tailored to a Young Living business, encouragement for the climb, two powerful scripts to train your team and your leaders with Oola principles, and a printable action sheet to help you apply all these tips once you put this book down. Are you ready?

The Best 40 Time Management Tips for A Young Living Business

I am not going to tell you how to order your day, because that's based on your personality type and what you're comfortable committing to. You may feel more on your game if you budget out every hour. Or you may prefer having blocks of similar tasks with spaces of free time. You may be far more productive with a handful of 20-minute business blitzes throughout your day. You may work with a pencil and paper planner. Or you may do it all digitally. The *"system"* is not as important as consistency and a few key time management ideas for specifically running a Young Living business. Let's blast through the ideas below. Pick one way and stick with it. Then do your list with deliberation and purpose every day.

Why do we procrastinate, and how do we stop it? Margie Warrell wrote this in Forbes magazine:

"The core of the discomfort is fear. That potent and instinctive emotion whose reason for being is to protect us from pain (including the emotional variety) and urge us away from anything it perceives might threaten our sense of self, injure our pride, or rattle our world. However, left unchecked, those fears can drive us to cling on to the hope that if we procrastinate long enough, our situation will improve, or our misgivings will magically evaporate and be replaced with newfound clarity and courage. We tell ourselves that 'one day' we will be ready to make a change or take a chance; that 'one day' the timing will be better, our confidence stronger, our circumstances easier.

"Unfortunately, the reverse is generally true. As the days roll steadily by, our fears grow larger, not smaller, until they eventually lead to a burial ground for unfulfilled dreams and untapped potential. All the time, our procrastination can exact a steep toll on our finances, career, business, relationships and health. We are loath to admit it, but in electing to put off today what can be done tomorrow, we

inadvertently sell out on our happiness."

I am a master procrastinator! I know that place SO well. Here are some of the things that I did to pull myself out of it. *(And I say pull because every day is still is a struggle!)* Procrastination is not a beast that you slay once and move on — it must be fought again and again, daily and weekly and sometimes hourly.

Get oils
ON AND IN YOUR
B O D Y
BEFORE YOU EVER START
Your Day

Tip 1: Oil Immediately

One of the biggest mistakes I see among Young Living leaders is that they don't oil frequently enough or use enough oil when they do break open the bottle. Some of the least-used oils in all of Young Living are the emotional oils, and the Oola oils fall under that category. Before you pray, get Oola Balance going in your diffuser and lean over it. Put some Oola Grow in your hands and cup them over your nose and take three deep breaths. Breathe out twice as slow as you breathe in. Get some of the Infused 7 oils on your feet based on your Oola wheel and the areas you're working on. Get oils on and in your body before you ever start your day. Do it again just before you fall asleep.

Tip 2: Start Your Day With God

That may mean losing yourself for five minutes in Scripture or praying over your day with your spouse at breakfast. When your day starts with Christ, you have given Him your first fruits. And it sets the pace and tone for the entire day. Try it for seven days and see how it goes!

Some of my favorite prayers include: wisdom on the planning of my day, the ability to see what to delegate, Solomon wisdom on financial and time management decisions, OGV growth *(and give a specific goal for the month)*, a strong Essential Rewards base *(and give a number)*, leaders with certain personalities on specific legs, leaders with initiative, and God's will over my business.

Tip 3: The Night Before, Or At The Start Of Your Day, Take 10 Minutes To Plot Out The Three Most Important Things Of The Day

I actually keep two lists — a long-form list with all the tasks I need to do, and a tiny three-item list just for that day. Then I am not overwhelmed, but I also have a solid list for the all the things I can't accomplish that day. Many use a whiteboard for this and order their day by number of importance. Some color code it and number it by task or difficulty. The OolaGuys use a simple 3x5 postcard. Whatever system you use, stick with the system. If a long list overwhelms you, make short ones. If a minute-by-minute bulletpoint is too much, build your schedule in chunks. Some set aside specific days every week for certain tasks. For example, on Tuesdays from 10-11 a.m., they do all their follow up for the week. On Wednesdays from 7-8 p.m., they do a Facebook Live and train their team. Every Thursday night at 6 p.m. they teach a class, either at home or for a team member. Set certain patterns if it helps you to have a routine. I will tell you that routines allow your team to follow what you're doing. If they expect you to be on every Wednesday at 7 p.m., you're a lot more likely to have a larger audience because you are consistent.

Tip 4: Stop Thinking and Start Doing

We spend so much time thinking about what we need to do that we don't actually do it. Instead of doodling about it and writing it in paragraph form, give yourself a couple word bulletpoints, close your planner and start crossing things off the list. Don't get paralysis by analysis. Get an idea of what you need and get started.

Tip 5: Don't Get Distracted

This is the hardest of all the tips, and on some days, it will be downright impossible. Don't beat yourself up if it's a high distraction day. But I will also tell you this: keeping your eye out for distractions will help you be more prepared. It's easier to say no when you are braced for them. By distractions, I mean children, random phone calls or instant messages, visitors, Facebook or any social media, or mundane tasks that aren't on your list. Distraction is the biggest enemy to your clock. You come out the victor by setting good boundaries. I once had a leader stand outside on my porch instead of walking in the door, because I knew the drop-in visit would go long, and I had only 20 minutes to get a nap before a night of being a mom taxi. It's ok to draw boundaries. Build in breaks if you get off your schedule so you can make up the time. Be willing to toss the schedule occasionally if you're having a tough day. But don't let every day become a tough day.

Tip 6: You Don't Have Much Time. Make the Minutes Matter

What does that mean? If you have blocked out thirty minutes to market a class, don't read web articles for 12 minutes and text a few friends first. Start right away. If you have one hour a day for your business *(which is absolutely enough time to grow a Diamondship),* give it the full 60 minutes. Don't lose half your time on non-income producing tasks. Give yourself a break when you hit a goal, but get started right away. The most valuable time you have is the first few minutes you start.

Tip 7: Delegate, Even To Your Kids And Leaders

What does this look like? I have one of my Silvers tally all my contests monthly. *(I am a blue personality. I like fun. I am math challenged.)* I recognize that tallying is not my strength, and she is very good at it. Here's another example. I make up 100 purple bags at the start of each month to carry on me in case I have an oils encounter. 80 % of your business is simply being prepared. In that bag I have instructions on how to order, a photo of the kit, a 101 class on cd, a Your Gameplan mini to show the business opportunity, and Fearless, to train the lifestyle. There are instructions on how to assemble them at oilabilityteam. com/follow-up-bags. Instead of assembling them all my-self, I engage my kids to sit at the dining room table once a month in an assembly line. Then we do something fun af-terward, like make ice cream or have a family movie night as a thank you. They contribute to our family business, and it saves me quite a bit of time assembling them. If they are older, I pay teenage kids $20 to put together mailings and purple bags! I carry purple bags everywhere so I'm not caught without tools. Delegation is a major time saving tool. Hire out your weaknesses. Even my elementary school kids get tasks! I strongly dislike doing follow up mailings. So I bless a local mom in our town with a few hours a week of paid work and it gets it off my plate. She makes enough to cover her essential rewards order, and I save time to put it into things I'm passionate about.

Tip 8: If Your Time Is Extremely Limited (Two Hours A Week Or Less), Focus On One Thing And One Thing Alone: Teach Classes

What does that mean? You can't find leaders if you don't teach. You can't get people on essential rewards if you don't teach. That means the number one income producing activity of all the activities out there you can spend your time on is sharing oils. If you have time for only one thing, make that your one thing. You can grow a large organization organically even if this is all you do. If leaders need to be trained, I point them to the Gameplan series. To get an essential rewards base, I point them to the Fearless book and print off a free Fearless calendar at oilabilityteam.com/fearless to complete ten challenges and learn the lifestyle. Those two tasks can be utilized sim-ply by pointing them to the tools. But teaching classes is all on you. If you have a very small check, take that check for the first six months and put it in your gas tank — and teach classes. Go where you know people. If that's the only thing you do until you can get enough freedom to do more, that one step will be enough. If you're overwhelmed with how little time you have, always start from that one place. Focus on teaching and nothing else.

Tip 9: Let The Small Stuff Go

If you're in a season of your life that's very demanding and busy, you may not be able to do some things on your wish list. You may not be able to send thank you's to every person who has been on Essential Rewards for a year or recognize Oiliversaries *(oil anniversaries)* or leader's birthdays. You may not be able to offer individualized coaching to your leaders or take them out for lunches or do recognition dinners. You may not be able to handle a lot of time consuming mailings.

You may need to stick to teaching classes, getting people on essential rewards and training your leaders until the crazy season is over. And if crazy is going to last a long time, then you'll get really good at skipping all the extras and going for growth. The rest is amazing, but not necessary. Stay laser-focused on growth *(in network marketing terms we call this IPAs — Income Producing Activities)* if you don't have a lot of time. Do the same task for the whole month on one day. For example, make a months' worth of purple bags in one sitting or pack up your mailers at once. Do all your coaching in a one-hour setting with back to back phone calls. Tighten your clock with similar activities.

Tip 10: Don't Try To Be Perfect

This is a tough one. Keep this in mind: there is a vast difference between excellence and perfection. I don't believe we can ever achieve perfection. There's only one Person on the earth that has ever accomplished that! I deal with this frustration in the newsroom every single time I anchor. If I just had another 40 seconds, I could put the spit and polish on my final story! But my time is up, I am live, and the story has to run as-is. Do each task to the point where a leader could copy it, or it serves its purpose. If you have time at the end of your tasks to go back and tweak it, then give yourself the freedom to do more. But not until the list is done. Excellence over perfection. Done is better than perfect!

Tip 11: Small, Consistent Tasks Pay Off More Than A Few Days Of Hustle

How did I get to Diamond? What specifically did I do from starter kit to freedom? I read the same script 288 times. We hit Diamond in February of 2017, after my 289th class. I didn't have a big friend circle — I was completely broke, and I lived in the middle of nowhere. I just read that script over and over and over again in front of new faces each week — anyone that would listen to the sound of my voice. Was it the Gameplan script that got me there? Heck, the script definitely works — I have had very high kit sales with it. But the real method to my madness was consistency. If I'd taught a class a month, or a class every other month, I would not have had the same results. It was a deliberate two-hour class every single week that got me that rank. A few days of hustle at the end of the month to try to jump rank is not sustainable. You lose rank with the next month, because it was not built on a solid foundation. You didn't take the time to train the lifestyle — you sold a kit. You didn't build the relationship, you pointed to 11 bottles of oil and a diffuser. That relationship and the knowledge of the lifestyle come a conversation at a time, a question at a time, through consistent deliberate investment. If you want longevity in your business, you need to work it with purpose every single week. That's how you get results that last.

Tip 12: Don't Put The Expectation On Your Spouse To Carry The Load. This Is Your Jam! It's Your Business

Does that mean they don't make a meal every now and then or take the kids so you can teach? No, not at all. If you have their support, ask them. If you don't, then earn their respect by showing them the check first. My kids came with me to just about all my classes when I first started. But also recognize that your spouse may not be there to bail you out if you have poor time management. They may not be catching up on your mailings for you or making follow up calls. This is your business. You began it. Just as you would not go to their workplace and do the job they do 40 hours a week, don't expect them to do that for you just because your business is based at home. Simply manage your clock better.

Also -- set at least two dates each month with your spouse. Don't talk about the business at either of them. No kids are allowed. It may be a date to the library or to the grocery store, but it counts if you are alone. It doesn't need to be expensive. But always make time to connect without the business. Your marriage has to take priority as you budget your time. Your marriage always trumps work.

Tip 13: Avoid Guilt By Protecting Sacred Circles

This is a bit of a new concept, but it's something I have been practicing at home in my own head ever since I became a working mom 20 years ago. Know your sacred circles. They change constantly! Evaluate weekly what's most important that week. What are sacred circles? It's an area of your life that you'd cry over if it was missed. Those get the first parts of your day. During our school year, homeschooling is a sacred circle. My phone is off and my undivided attention goes on my kids. There are no calls with leaders at 10 a.m. — that is disrespectful to my kids. In the summer, one of my sacred circles is my body, as I cleanse and give myself extra rest and a longer workout each day. On Sundays, a sacred circle is church. Those circles will change with the ebb and flow of your year. But make sure you have your life in the right order, or you'll develop a bitterness for the business as important things get missed. Those circles are filled in first, then the business comes after. Your life should be in this order: God, spouse, kids, work *(Young Living)*. If your priorities are in check, the rest will fall into place, even when it seems like there is no space for it. Have certain boundaries that will not be crossed.

Tip 14: Build Respect For Your Business In Your Family

When you are at your regular job, they do not walk in and take over. For example, when I was anchoring, my kids knew if they even whispered in the studio as I spoke to millions of people, they were in serious trouble. I could lose my job. The same line of respect needs to be drawn for your home-based business. You'll never see my kids when I am doing a Facebook live — because they know they lose all electronics, all cell phones and all freedom if they cross that line. It's a no-disobey zone. We respect the regular workplace, but once we bring a business home — all the rules are off. But in the same breath — my kids know that when it's their time, that time belongs to them. And the business does not cross it. I give them the same respect when the business is off that they give me when the business is on. It's a mutual trust relationship. If you build that training into your business from the beginning, there are fewer interruptions and distractions.

Tip 15: Recognize That There Are Hustle Months And There Are Growth Months

They are not the same thing. Admittedly, there will be times when you have to hustle. Those months require a bit more work and a few more hours than what you usually put in. You're up for a rank up that month. You're running a rally or a leader's retreat. But here's the ultimate goal: growth. Not every month is a hustle month. But every month should be a growth month. If you're not growing, you're not doing the business successfully. That takes consistency in the small parts of your day, day after day. A young living business is not built in a month. It takes months and years of tenacity and steadiness.

Tip 16: Don't Skip Sleep

Or working out. Or a healthy snack instead of junk food. Or a 10-minute power clean of the house. You'll feel worlds better when you start. Self-care is SO important. It's the *"why"* behind a Young Living lifestyle of wellness, purpose, and abundance. You can't draw a team with a lifestyle you don't own. The little bits of time you use to make good healthy choices for your body will help you to focus and feel stronger when you are working. You are what you eat; don't put yuck in your mouth.

Tip 17: How Do I Find The Time??

Instead of trying to *'find'* extra time, make better use of the time you already have. What is stealing your time? Critically take 24 hours and look at your day as if you were looking from the outside in. Are there places where you can trim the fat? Are there moments where your brain rests that you can fill with something purposeful? Can you have more self-control in putting kids to bed or rising earlier to utilize portions of your day that are lost?

Finding time for my business was not a quick fix. With a full time 4 a.m. high-stress job, 6 hours of homeschooling each day, kid's activities, cooking gluten, sugar and dairy free, raising an autistic son, and collapsing to 5 or 6 hours of sleep every night — none of that gave me a leg up on *"finding"* time. There was NO space. What did I do? I dialed everything back just a smidge. Maybe it was only 5 minutes, but each part of my day lost a few minutes. And those few minutes gave me 20 minutes in my afternoon to work the business as I was just starting. That 20 minutes, became a more disciplined 30, then 45, then 60 – and as a Diamond, I can take a full 2 hours in the afternoon now if I need it. If I do not, I get a lazy afternoon nap. That simple act of pulling back each area of your life just a little will make just enough room for something that can bless your family for generations.

Tip 18: Break Your Day Into Tiny Chunks

What do you do if you can't focus for long periods of time? Do two or three 20-minute power blocks. Start the egg timer and hunker down until 2 follow up calls are made, or a few posts scheduled to market a class – then when the buzzer goes off at 20 minutes, put it all away, stop the hustle and enjoy your afternoon. You made it. Power sessions are great if you have small kids, are adrenally done, or have a hard time focusing for long periods of time. It helps with this system to group like things together: follow up calls, mailings, coaching sessions, training your brain, etc....

Tip 19: Put Everything In Your Planner And Don't Make Any Commitments Until You Check It First

It helps to color code things as well, green for Young Living, orange for family, etc... This avoids embarrassing double-booking sessions. (By the way – the Oola oils are color coded as a reminder for the key areas of life). Color coding also helps you to space out responsibilities, so you don't overwhelm yourself, because you can see it on the page. Also, engage in purposeful scheduling. Always look a minimum of 2 weeks ahead. Make sure you schedule time to schedule and fill out your planner, even if that time falls on a weekend with less responsibilities or a quiet weeknight evening.

Tip 20: This Goes Hand In Hand With The Planner: Have Some Strategy To Your Business

What do I mean by that? I spent a year putting together the Gameplanner to keep you accountable and laser-focused on the three things that grow your business — including three business tasks a day, follow up pages to track mailings, rank mapping sheets so you can see which legs you need to be teaching under and how many classes you are from your next rank, and stat tracking in 8 month increments so you can know your weaknesses before they hit you, like a drop in Essential Rewards percentages or the amount of new members added each month. If you have some strategy heading into your month, you know where to place your time, which leaders to focus on, and where to teach. It is invaluable in decision making so you're not wasting a second. By having a strategy and knowing the stats of your business, you go into each day knowing how your time should be spent, and what the most important tasks are for that day.

Tip 21: Utilize Seemingly Useless Moments Of Your Day: Streamline

Practice the 101 script when you are in the shower. Practice your story. Run your Savvy class while you are applying your makeup and practice what you are applying. Make follow up calls on lunch if you have a job, or on the way home from work, or during breaks! Make calls during your drive time and train your brain then, too. Utilize podcasts — they are underused! Listen on your cell phone! Youtube's Jim Rohn trainings are some of my favorite. There are over 70 oilabilityteam.com free podcast interviews and textable classes that, with one click on your cell phone, you can send to people who say they can't make class — and they can listen to an entire 101 on their phone.

I also made a commitment to check social media while I'm walking on my treadmill! It actually makes me look forward to exercising! It's amazing how fast a 30-minute walk goes while walking on the treadmill and looking at social media. It's my *"reward"* for a day of hard work.

Facebook Live is a huge time saver as well. Train your team over Facebook lives instead of traveling. As your team gets larger, it's more efficient to do more and more of your training online. Allow other leaders on your team to stand in for you if you do weekly trainings — because it allows those on the team to connect with other leadership styles and hear other stories of success *(and it gives you a week of rest)*. In network marketing, we call that social proof — they can see other's stories and believe it for themselves.

Finally, just for sanity, bedtime is non-negotiable. The kids are in bed by 8:30 every night, so that bedtime is usually a smooth, routine process. Then I can get some work done starting at 9 p.m., with good peace & quiet. I also get up earlier than my kids to get a few moments in the morning that are uninterrupted.

Tip 22: Set Reasonable Boundaries And Don't Overextend Yourself

Burnout is real! Schedule rest. Prioritize wisely. If your list is too long, you won't know where to start and will feel defeated before you even begin. Taking a rest will increase your productivity. Tired, overworked minds do not make good decisions quickly or retain information efficiently. If you get tired, learn to rest, not to quit. Don't focus on yesterday. If it was an off day, don't sweat it. Today is what counts. You can make it memorable or let it slip by. Also, don't recreate the wheel. Don't waste your time making your own version of tools that have already been created. That is sweat equity you don't need to generate. No Diamondship is worth your health. We have a saying among the Diamonds called *"Diamond coma"* after you hit rank the first time. Some get lost in it for a full six months, recuperating from their intense hustle to rank for the first time. Pace yourself and avoid burnout.

Tip 23: Make Double Batches Of Dinner

I only cook 3-4 times a week. Then we eat leftovers for a couple of meals. One or two days a week, I hand the responsibility of cooking to my teenagers. One unexpected benefit to this: my teens now know how to cook!

Tip 24: Prioritize Your Tasks Based On Results

Don't do all the easy stuff, start with the hardest tasks first. Do the worst first! Focus on one thing at a time. Always prioritize tasks in order of the net result or you'll be tempted to procrastinate the hard stuff but still feel *"busy"* but not doing things that bring the most results. Once you start on a project, finish what you were doing before starting something else. You're much more likely to finish the hard jobs if you begin with them when you have the most energy.

Tip 25: Give Yourself The First And Last Half 15 Minutes Of Your Day

You can use it as down time, or you can use it to organize — whatever helps you feel best prepared and grounded. If you prefer to organize the last hour of your day then thank God for an amazing day. Pray and read your Bible and be still to hear God's still, small voice speaking to you. Be sure that what you're taking on is given to you and guided by the Holy Spirit because He won't lead you into being overbooked with something you aren't destined or gifted to do. Leave room for the Lord to change your plans.

Tip 26: Have Your Home In Order And Picked Up

Even if it's not exactly 'clean', having it clutter-free and everything in its place lifts such a burden off my shoulders! I feel like I have extra time to get other things accomplished!

Do a 10-minute power clean in the morning and again at night with all your kids to straighten common areas, or, at the very least, your workspace — so you have one clean spot where you can focus.

Tip 27: Keep A Note Pad Beside Your Bed

Every night, list the three most important things to do tomorrow. After they are done, THEN give yourself a reward. It's a huge stress reliever to have a notepad by my bed so I know I won't lie in bed hoping I don't forget something that came to mind. Make sure you don't switch notebooks by accident! Keep your notebook close.

Tip 28: Unplug

I give myself one social media day of rest each week to clock out and focus on family. The Oola guys do this too! Take a Sabbath. God set the example of resting on the 7th day not because He needed rest, but because we needed rest and he wanted us to follow His pattern. In addition to unplugging, I plug my phone in on the other side of my bedroom. Then when my alarm goes off, I have to get up. I also plug it in at a set time each night, so I don't lay there half-asleep scrolling and wonder where two hours went. In the morning, make your bed so you're not tempted to get back in it. Also, in the morning, I do one thing for my business or my home before I allow myself to look at my phone.

Tip 29: Utilize Young Living products!

Nitro. Mindwise. NingXia. Brain Power or Geneyus or Angelica in the diffuser. That is my go-to combo for worktime. I love Pure Protein Complete in a smoothie for brain food. I also firmly believe in Oola Grow and Oola Balance in my diffuser and on my feet at night before bed. I'll give you an entire Oola oils protocol in the scripts at the back of this book.

Tip 30: Practice Setting Boundaries

It's ok to say no. Be willing to go out of bounds for things the Lord has for you that may not fit into your plan. Keep praying for the wisdom and discernment to know which things you need to focus on and which things you can discard OR just wait for a better time. Saying *"No"* has been hard for me because I like to be all things for everyone but me. When you have less on your plate, you are able to spend more time completing tasks and you produce better quality work. Turn off notifications on your phone — that's a boundary that requires a lot of self-control. Set a timer when you are on social media to remind yourself to get off. I do this with phone calls, too! With a team of thousands, you could give every minute of your day away without good boundaries.

Tip 31: Put Your Keys, Wallet, Sunglasses, Water Bottle, Starter Kit In A Bag, And Other Items In The Same Place Every Time You Get Home

Store them somewhere near the door or where it makes sense for you to easily grab and go as you leave. Hunting for stuff is a huge waste of time. It's the same thing with business tools. Put purple bags in your car and in your purse, roll ons with carrier oils strategically in your cabinets, purse and glove compartment. Collect a few bins with paper, tape, scissors, box cutters, pens, etc... in your business supplies area. Place oils where you will use them: Pan Away by your bedside, Stress Away in your van with an orb diffuser, and Vitality oils in the kitchen. Lay things out so they are easy to use. It is a time saver. 80 % of oiling is simply putting them in your path. Your kids will learn to reach for them first if they see you doing it also. Make it easy on yourself by with strategic placement.

Tip 32: Communicate With Your Spouse Or Partner (In Advance) About Time You May Need To Be Uninterrupted

You may need them to clean up dinner or take care of the kids so you can teach a class or have some time to connect with your team online. Communication in the home helps tremendously to make the time spent truly effective.

Tip 33: Be Willing To Make Sacrifices

Stop watching TV, dial back on friendships that mentally or emotionally drain you, order your groceries so you're not mindlessly wandering aisles at the store, use kid's birthday parties and other social events as prospecting events *(use your oils and let them ask you questions)*, and teach for everyone who will let you. That is the fastest way to get from A to B. Put your phone in airplane mode when you are power housing through a task so you don't lose your focus.

Tip 34: Stop Gathering More Info, More Knowledge, And More Education

You know enough to execute the basic income-producing tasks in your business. Every day, do at least one basic income-producing activity *(teach classes, get people on essential rewards, train your leaders).* Stop watching and listening to *"how to's"* for hours, days, and weeks and just start to DO them. Allow hustle time. You need a three-page Gameplan script and a starter kit to blow up your business. Just move your feet and spend time with people. Share your passion. That's the best way possible that you can spend your time in this business.

Tip 35: Follow Your Body's Cues

If your best mental clarity is at 7 a.m. or 7 p.m., do the tasks that use your brain a little more at those hours. That might include organizing and completing paperwork, writing emails, picking up the phone and doing follow up or doing online marketing for a class. Save mundane tasks for the end of your day.

Tip 36: If You Are Tech Savvy, Use Time Checking Apps

Some of my favorites are:

- **Any.do (task management cell phone app),**
- **Clear** (a chunking app that allows you to categorize goals and syncs with your iCloud account),
- Asana (allows you to share your progress on certain tasks with a group of people),
- **Dragon Naturally Speaking** (allows you to dictate letters, email messages or reports and send them to your computer or phone),
- **Rescuetime** (helps you report breaks you take, websites you visit, apps you use, and helps you stay on track with productivity goals),
- **Unroll.me** (allows you to unsubscribe from email you don't want).
- **Facebook scheduling** or **Hootesuite** to schedule on multiple sites.
- Jake Dempsey's **Project Broadcast** app to send mass text messages to your downline.
- **Cinchshare** to get all your posts scheduled for at least a week out,
- **Marco Polo** to keep in touch with your team.
- The **Priority Matrix** app is also amazing, it has a great system that allows leaders to work on projects together.
- Use a **Google Calendar** that you share with a common email address.
- **Teamzy.com** is good for managing relationships and staying in touch with people consistently.

Tip 37: Keep A Poster Of Your Whys (Your Reasons For Doing The Business) Front And Center

Place it somewhere that you can see it several times a day. It might be in the visor of your car or on your bathroom mirror. Include affirmations over your life and Scriptures that speak to you. Affirmations may sound a bit weird, but it's just the concept of speaking life over yourself. Whatever negative thoughts you have, write down the opposite. One of your biggest obstacles in this business isn't the time on the clock, it's getting your head in the right place to even want to utilize the time you have been given.

Tip 38: Do Not Multi-Task

Finish what you start before beginning the next thing on your list. Our brains do not multitask, as parallel processors in a computer do, even though we think we can do two things at once. It takes less time to start, finish, and start another task than to do two tasks concurrently. There is one exception to this rule, and that's if you're not doing something brain intensive. Many a leader has trained their brain while driving by listening to cd's, or by watching videos while they run on a treadmill, or listening to podcasts as they wash dishes. I'm talking about working on a mailing during a phone call. Finish a task, or you may end up with a package going to the wrong person! There is a lot of science stacked against multi-tasking. Neuroscientist Earl Miller says you're not actually doing two things at once, you are switching between both of them very rapidly in your brain. He says writing an email and talking on the phone are nearly impossible to do simultaneously.

Tip 39: Give In To Small Indulgences

Set a goal for yourself for being disciplined and having self-control. Perhaps when you hit Executive, you will take $100 of your check each month and invest in 1 delivered meal from Sun Basket or Thrive Market. Maybe you will get a cleaning lady for $50 a week. *(That was the best $200 a month I've ever spent in my LIFE. My floors are mopped every week!)* If you are faithful with the small things, the Lord will make you ruler over more. Small goals are good to reach the finish line. Time yourself. Put pressure on yourself to get it done in a short amount of time instead of prolonging the item on the list having it take too much time.

Tip 40: Release Yourself From End-Of-Day Guilt

We tend to sit down at the end of the day and get frustrated that we didn't have time to play Legos with one of our littles or go on a one-hour run. Don't do that!! Something inside me says if Jesus was sitting there, he wouldn't be beating us up for the stuff we did not get to at the end of the day. Get through your list of three, then give yourself the freedom to play, without guilt. If you miss a play day or two, tighten the number of things on the list or the amount of time you give yourself to do them so you always have a chance to catch your breath. Do everything in moderation. When I have certain tasks that need to be done, I make a check list and assign various little rewards to myself for when I accomplish them, and I have to complete them in a set amount of time. The best way to get me moving is to make it a competition against myself. The minute you see something as a chore, that's when you start procrastinating.

What Now??

You did it! You made it past the top tips to manage your clock in a Young Living business. These words of wisdom will give you a life of less stress, more balance, and greater purpose... an Oola life. When one spoke of the wheel is out of whack, you will feel it in all the other areas of your life. Own your work.

Only schedule 80% of your time - not just your business time - but your entire life. This leaves room for impromptu moments of fun. It also leaves space for emergencies. It's a good rule of thumb to have some blank spaces on the calendar.

It's ok to have boundaries. Ask yourself if you can do the task. Is it helpful? Will it help you reach your goal? Say yes or say no, but don't feel guilty about your decision. It's part of your task to balance your clock.

Let me pause here and give you some very specific things that I did as I was growing my Young Living business to Diamond. It took me a little over two and a half years to go from my Starter Kit to a Diamondship. There were nights I did not get to stay up late and watch a family movie, because I knew I needed rest to anchor the next morning then teach a class that night. Part of it was sacrifice.

The first six months, I put my paycheck in my gas tank and went where I knew people. I did not have a large friend circle — I had just moved from Chicago, 750 miles away. That tells me you don't need a big friend circle to pull this off. You just need a few on-fire oilers that are willing to open their doors so you can teach to their friends. I found those by building relationships — finding out needs and meeting them where they were. I didn't build my business off another business or from social media *(though there are many Diamonds that have had tremendous success with both of those)* — my story was just a simple one of a script and a circle of friends on a couch.

When I look at what actually grew my team, it was steady, consistent teaching. That's why I'm ending this book with two scripts. You grow by sharing. Take those scripts and train. Everyone, whether they are doing the business or not, needs balance in their life. Everyone feels mediocre at something they are responsible for. Meet them in that place. I have given you the words to say, if only you will share.

I dialed back other areas of my life to find space to teach. Some weeks it was lunch with a friend. Many days it was social media time. Sometimes it was an earlier bedtime or an earlier rising time. Sometimes my run was just a little bit shorter, my dinner just a hair tighter, my makeup in the morning a few minutes less. If you shave a smidge here and there, you find that you have the breathing room to teach. It's not an enormous commitment — my classes usually run about two hours, and that's with time to build relationships included.

I made the decision to go for the business even when I was tired. Most adults I know are tired. You can't use that as the crutch to put the stop button on your business. Because if you do, you'll never get to a place where you can find rest. I truly own and dictate my clock now. I am my own boss. I set my hours. I built my paycheck. But it was only with self-control and discipline, and a willingness to teach a class once a week — no matter my level of exhaustion, the things on my plate, or my distractions. Those are all excuses. Every Diamond in Young Living has battled the same battles — but they got there because they never gave up. They taught when it was hard.

I want you to take a highlighter when you are done reading this book, and go back through the top 40 time saving tips, and highlight the 5 that spoke to you the most. Give it a week and implement them. See if it helps you carve a few more minutes out of your day.

Then look at the calendar for the next month and get 4 classes on it — one class a week. Commit to having discipline throughout your day so you can get to those classes faithfully. If you look at your calendar and there is nothing scheduled next month, you're not looking at a rank up month. Remember the income disclosure statement at the start of this book? That's YOU. That's your life. That's what's coming. It's on the way. But not if you stay where you are.

Let me recap the top things that got me to Diamond:

- giving up small pleasures to make way for two hours a week to teach

- putting my paycheck in my gas tank for six months to go where my friends were and sharing
- practicing the three-page Gameplan 101 script and getting it in front of anyone that would listen
- dialing back some of the routines of my day (length of breakfast, etc...) to find more minutes for the business
- doing income producing activities even when I was tired
- banning excuses from my lips
- making a commitment to teach classes even when it was hard
- scheduling 4 classes a month, even if they are only with one person
- having self-control to let things go if they are not perfect
- being disciplined. One of my favorite verses in scripture is 1 Corinthians 9:24-27: *"Do you not know that those who run in a race all run, but one receives the prize? Run in such a way that you may obtain it. And everyone who competes for the prize is temperate in all things. Now they do it to obtain a perishable crown, but we for an imperishable crown. Therefore I run thus: not with uncertainty. Thus I fight: not as one who beats the air. But I discipline my body and bring it into subjection."*

That doesn't sound like it's easy, right? It's not. You may have ten thousand hard choices between where you are now and your Diamondship. But aren't 10,000 choices better than the possibility of standing where you are now... forever? Isn't freedom worth it?

Here is the secret to this entire book: time management is not about lacking time. It is lacking a compelling reason to act. The matter is not important enough for you to respond promptly. Time management is reflecting what's inside your heart. You have to wake up knowing why you're pursuing this business, or you won't fight for it. If you have discipline, just about any goal is attainable. Keep your eyes on where you are going, pursue activities that will get you there, and get your feet moving with passion every day that there's breath in your lungs. Wake up with excitement, joy, and gratitude at this precious gift that you have been given of wellness, abundance, and purpose through Young Living. Freedom is on the other side, if only you will not give up.

Do you remember the beginning of the story? I was the worn news anchor that couldn't keep my car on the road. I was the mom of five from the projects. I've spent more of my life out of balance than in it. I've spent decades chasing things that were important to me, never feeling adequate and never getting ahead. I was the weary one that had nothing for her children.

All that has changed.

It wasn't the Diamondship that changed my life. It was the decision to be disciplined. It was the choice to live an Oola life. Every time you start to make an excuse, ask yourself why. There is no Diamondship without self-control, discipline, and balance. You'll lose your rank as fast as you gain it, even if you're a rockstar at enrolling. You can't hold on to something you have not mastered. Your marriage will suffer, your family will suffer, your finances will suffer, your health will suffer, and you'll feel it in all other areas of your life if you cannot dictate how you spend the minutes of your day. Evaluate your Oola wheel. Master the time management skills needed to reign in your day. And hold yourself accountable with the Oola for Business worksheet one week at a time, one day at a time, one hour at a time if need be. Time is a precious blessing. It's your task to be the steward.

Is it Worth the Work?

I look back over the last forty years of my life, and I'm so thankful I never gave up. I'm thankful that I didn't look at the task of the juggling the plates and stand down, overwhelmed. There were so many hard days! And many times, I have dropped more than I carried. It's normal to feel that way. But if you never fight for this, you'll never get to experience the thrill of peace. The ability to rest. Or the freedom of financial stress lifted. You'll never see freedom for your team as they follow your lead. You'll never get a full breath of air in your lungs and know that you have built a willable income, payable to your children for generations because of the work of your hands — because of your diligence, tenacity and self-control.

Take these last few moments and imagine what freedom looks like for you. See yourself standing in it. Believe in the deepest parts of your mind that you have what it takes to go all the way. Picture yourself as a Royal Crown Diamond. Breathe freedom for just a few seconds! Know that you can master delegation, boundaries, and saying no. You have an incredible path ahead! You have a hope and a future beyond your wildest dreams.

It's time to walk. It's time to fight. It's time to live the Oola life.

Oola Infused 7 Tea Party Script
by Young Living Diamond Sarah Harnisch

Script Only: 56 minutes, plus 11 minutes of video
Script + Tea Time: 90 minutes to 2 hours

Prior to class, begin diffusing Oola Grow. Set up a tea station complete with OolaTea and Vitality oils. Prep your TV or computer to show the five Oola videos. As attendees arrive, hand them an Oola mini and instruct them to turn to the pages of the wheel. Allow 15 minutes to fill out the questionnaire and personal OolaWheels. At the end of class, give them the printable at oolalife.org/gameplan or oilabilityteam.com/oola so they have an Oola system once they leave.

Intro

Welcome everyone! Thank you for taking time to hang with me and study Oola oils and tea! This will be a fast-paced fun class to train you how to utilize Young Living oils and to find more balance in your life. By the time you walk out of here, you'll have a good handle on the areas you need to key into, and I'll give you tools to help you focus as you juggle all those plates in the air. Much like a circus performer spins several plates, we have home, life, career, and so much more. It can be overwhelming. The number one thing I hear is that you wish you could clone yourself! There is no cloning essential oil — but this is about as close as we can get. It's about focus, priorities, lower stress, and more balance. Everyone feels mediocre at something. Everyone feels overwhelmed. Everyone feels they need more time in their day. This class meets you in that place. This is the what-to-do-when-you're-there class. Let's make oils the first thought and not the afterthought.

Let's start by introducing you to a few people. Dr. Troy Amdahl (@OolaGuru) and Dr. Dave Braun (@OolaSeeker) are the OolaGuys. They wrote an international best-selling book series called Oola: Find Balance in an Unbalanced World. They are currently traveling around the United States in a vintage VW surf bus on the Oola Dream Tour inspiring hope by collecting one million dreams and providing one million meals to children in need. Sarah Harnisch is an international speaker, Amazon best-selling author of the Gameplan series, news anchor, Young Living Diamond, and homeschooling mom of five. She's the author of the Oola mini. Let's get to know them better!

(Video 1: Oola intro video, 2 minutes)

Note, if you do not have the videos, find them at oolalife.com/gameplan or oilabilityteam.com/oola. They are free. They can be downloaded and played on a tablet, computer, or cell phone. With the right cable, you can also hook your computer up to a television screen. If you do not have access to a way to play them, simply skip the opening paragraph to each video and read the script without the videos. The script can stand alone without them.

The OolaGuys and Sarah will be hanging with us for the whole class! I'm your host. My name is _____, and I am a *(rank)* in Young Living. *(Share your story: how you got involved with oils, your wow moment, what they mean to you. Why do you have passion to share oils?)*

Oola Grow is in the diffuser right now. It's a blend of 23 Young Living oils — six of them are not available as singles. This is my favorite oil for courage and to focus on the task at hand. It's my stay-on-track oil to encourage clarity of thought and action, personal growth, happiness and empowerment. Oola Grow promotes feelings of acceptance. It's AMAZING. *(Pass the oil around for them to smell).* As a side note...

Grow would work really well in the bedroom. You could rub it on your inner thighs before intimacy. It would increase blood flow and sensuality. It helps support an emotional connection with your partner.

From the bedroom back to BALANCE... since we have a lot to cover, I have great news for you! You get to take this whole experience home. The Oola mini book I gave you at the door is yours to keep — and this entire script I am speaking from is in the back of the book, so you can leave with it and read it all over again when you are alone.

What Is Oola?

Let's start at the very beginning. Oola is a life that is balanced and growing in the key areas of health, finances, career, relationships, and well-being. It can be a noun or a verb. It can be a destination or a feeling. It can be as complex as a life growing in fitness, finance, family, field *(career/ business)*, faith, friends, and fun *(the 7 F's of Oola)*, or as simple as a sunset, a quiet book on the beach, or a special moment with a child. It is that place we all shoot for in life.

It's time to take a peek at the OolaWheel you filled out when you first walked in the door. The OolaWheel points out your weakest link. It's a place to start. That's the oil I want you to focus on today as we train.

Let's talk about oils briefly first so you have a quick overview on how and why they work.

What Are Essential Oils?

They are the most powerful part of the plant. They are distilled from shrubs, flowers, trees, roots, bushes, fruit, rinds, resins and herbs. They consist of over 100 different natural, organic compounds. Some are steam distilled, some are resin-tapped, and some are cold pressed, but they all have an effect on the human body. There are three ways to use them: aromatically, topically, and internally. Young Living has an entire Vitality line of internal oils. None of the Oola oils are Vitality oils approved for internal use — so the protocols I give you today will be for aromatic or topical use. Founder Gary Young specifically formulated these blends for your nose.

The olfactory senses are the strongest and oldest centers of the brain to recall memory. The oils are formulated to anchor your goal to action and to your affirmation. They are designed to push out bad thoughts and bring in good thoughts.

Why use an oil? Does it actually work?? Scientifically speaking, absolutely. Oils are tinier than viruses — and have access to the limbic lobe of the brain, the emotional control center. That is why you will feel calm, happy, or at peace when you diffuse them. If you need the opposite of an emotion, the first place I turn is oils. I get them in my diffuser and breathe. If you don't have a lot of time, here's a simple aromatic protocol you can do in a few seconds without a diffuser.

Oola Oils Aromatic Protocol

1) Place 1 drop of oil in the palm of your hand. Turn the oil with the fingers of your other hand.

2) Say an affirmation before you start. Whatever doubt or fear is in your mind, think of the opposite. Use your OolaWheel to know your weakest places and start with those oils.

3) Put both hands together and cup them over your face and breathe in three times, as full as your lungs will go. Breathe out twice as slow as you breathe in.

4) Take a moment and put yourself into a state of gratitude today about where you are going.

5) Apply the remaining oil in your hand to the back of your neck and your wrists.

If you want to mix Oola Grow or Oola Balance with one of the Infused 7 oils *(whichever one you're working on that day),* place 1 drop of Grow or Balance in your palm with 3 drops of the Infused 7 oil. The ratio is 1:3, and you'll have a flawless blend. Both sets of oils were designed to work together.

One of the things that makes Young Living so amazing is the Seed to Seal promise. Seed to Seal is based on three pillars: sourcing, science, and standards. Young Living's oils are tested by scientists with over 180 years of combined lab experience. They do third party testing with two accredited, respected, independent labs.

Young Living is the global leader in essential oils, with over 1.5 billion dollars in sales annually. Those that use the oils keep coming back! There are three thousand global employees, 600 life changing products, 16 corporate and partner farms, 20 international markets, 50 highly trained scientists — most, hand-trained by Gary Young himself, and four million Young Living users. What does that mean? The testing is thorough and exact.

Why can't you just buy oils at the grocery store? Purity. You get what you pay for. I have seen bottles of Frankincense for $7 at the store, but it costs more than that just to distill! It's a red flag that the oil has been adulterated.

All oils in the world fall under four categories: authentic, manipulated, perfume or synthetic.

1) Authentic means the oils are 100 % pure, with no added synthetics or other species in the bottle. These are Young Living oils!

2) Manipulated means the final product has been made to smell more pleasing and less earthy. Some of the heavier molecules have been stripped out, or another species introduced, to enhance the aroma.

3) Perfume oils are not pure. They are mixed with synthetics to enhance the aroma. These oils have no therapeutic action. Frequently, solvents are used to extract from the plant.

4) Synthetic oils are not true oils at all. They smell nothing like the original plant and are typically labeled as *"scented products."* These are synthetic.

Authentic is the only true, pure oil. Synthetic oils would be like opening your fridge, taking a glass of orange juice, and diluting it 95 % before you drank it. It would not have the benefits of a full glass of orange juice. Young Living's Seed to Seal process is promise of integrity. There are no pesticides used, no artificial fertilizers, and no weed killers. The plants are harvested at their peak, then put through a vigorous testing process. They go from the farm to your home.

You're going to get to experience nine oils today — the Infused 7 kit and the first two oils that Gary formulated for Oola, Grow and Balance. *((Then I'll tantalize your tastebuds with some Vitality oils, perfectly blended with organic Oola tea. By the time you leave you'll be a pro — you will have tried oils aromatically, topically, and internally all in one sitting. That's very Oola!))*

(NOTE: the tea class begins here. If you wish to only cover oils, skip ahead to Video 4).

Let's pause and get you a refreshment for the second half of the class. We're about to kick this into high gear. It's time for a little OolaTea party. As I set up, watch this.

(Video 2: OolaTea backstory, 2 minutes)

(Bring out teacups with OolaTea and Vitality oils for each person).

People are buying beverages every day. Many are addicted to coffee, soda, and energy drinks. Tea is the 2nd most consumed drink in the world — behind water. 159 million cups of tea are consumed per day in the United States. OolaTea replaces their current beverage with a certified organic tea that's under $1 per serving and requires Vitality oils to complete the experience. We are paving the road for tea to be infused with Young Living oils. No one has ever done it before.

When we formulate tea blends, we start with the oils we want to use, then create the blend around that to make sure the support and taste will be dialed in. Every cup is perfectly scientifically formulated to perfectly pair with a Young Living Vitality oil.

Tea is one of the healthiest beverages on the planet because it is naturally loaded with antioxidants. It's been used for over 5,000 years and studied thoroughly for effectiveness. OolaTea is the only tea in the world that is certified organic whole leaf and is specifically formulated for essential oil infusion. It is one of the best ways to get the benefits of essential oils into your body.

Let's take this a step further. What if you could use organic OolaTea to detox your body? Ever heard of a green tea detox? Imagine the junk that you have put in your body over the last 365 days. Now, imagine a life where you woke up feeling less bloated, tired and achy, and more energetic, vibrant and healthy.

The 14-day Detox Challenge is designed to help you break addictions to sugar, coffee, and soda and energy drinks - while feeling healthier and losing weight! Dr. Dave Braun (@OolaSeeker) personally guides you through the entire 14-day detox process to help you live a healthier and more vibrant OolaLife. That's available for FREE at oolatea.com/detox.

Are You Ready To Taste And Learn About The Tea?

(If you only have one kind of tea, simply pass that around and talk about the rest. If you have several, allow them to try small samples. Note: Vitality oils are strong. Mix as directed on the packaging. More is not necessarily better! Vitality oils needed for ten of the most popular teas are: Peppermint, Clove, Bergamot, Lemongrass, Grapefruit, Cardamom, Black Pepper, Orange, and Lime. New tea blends are released every month! Find them at oolatea.com.)

1) Energy OolaTea (Peppermint Rush)

Organically grown in the foothills of the Himalayas, these silver-tipped leaves are among the finest Darjeeling boasts. With hints of French grapes and Himalayan mountain air, its musky-sweet taste sparks memories of a fine wine. Frequently referred to as the *"Champagne of Teas,"* Darjeeling is one of the most exquisite and sought-after teas in the world and provides the perfect base to pair with Peppermint Vitality essential oil. It's a rush that invigorates the body.

2) Detox OolaTea (Dragon Clove)

Resting peacefully in the shadows of the Longjing mountains are the elite plantations that produce the most high-end teas from China. Dragonwell tea, unfermented and clean, greets you with its jade hue and unforgettable aroma. Rich in antioxidants, Vitamin C and amino acids, and paired with the perfect Clove Vitality essential oil, this organic tea blend is ideal for fat burning, digestion, and is a natural anti-inflammatory.

3) Earl Grey OolaTea (Bergamot Black)

Legend has it that Lord Grey added bergamot to his daily tea to cover-up the lime taste in the local water. No longer a tea reserved for lords, this robust blend, with its crisp citrusy bouquet, is the perfect complement to a day filled with to-do lists, emails, and goals to be crushed. Infuse this Earl Grey base with Bergamot Vitality essential oil, and you hold in your hand the healthy fuel you need to face the world and go make your OolaLife happen. It's an energy boost, enhances mental clarity, and improves dental health.

4) Sleep OolaTea (Citrus Chamomile)

Delicious, calming and naturally caffeine-free, this Chamomile, hibiscus and orange peel tea is just one drop of Lemongrass Vitality essential oil away from completing the experience. This is the perfect tea to help unwind after a busy day and regain balance in your life. This tea improves sleep, supports healthy skin, and reduces stress.

5) Glow Oolong OolaTea (Oola Oolong)

History tells us of a man named Wu Liang who discovered Oolong tea by accident when distracted after a long day picking tea. By the time he returned to his tea, it had already started to oxidize and at that moment a new variety of tea was founded. At Oola, we don't believe in accidents. You will understand what we mean when you experience the healthy vibrant glow from this organic Oola Oolong blend. The full, toasty and warming aroma will awaken your senses and remind you that everything happens for a reason. With Grapefruit Vitality essential oil, this tea supports healthy skin, promotes weight loss, and prevents bone loss.

6) Peace OolaTea (Cinnamon Chai)

Lying on either side of the Brahmaputra River bordering Bangladesh and Myanmar lie the rich tea fields of Assam. The tea in this region is of the highest quality throughout

India. By combining this Assam black tea and Cardamom Vitality essential oil with the classic spices of cardamom pods, cinnamon pieces and ginger root, we get this warm, mysterious *"peace of mind"* blend. In a world filled with chaos, we can all benefit from a sip of *"peace"* in our day. This strengthens immunity, reduces bloating, and boosts metabolism.

7) Oxford OolaTea (Double Black)

Our traditional English blend includes only the finest golden-tipped Indian tea leaves resulting in a strong and malty flavor. This bold blend has broad appeal, whether as a stand-alone tea or go *"British style"* and indulge with a dash of milk and sugar. *"Double-up"* and add the recommended Black Pepper Vitality and Orange Vitality essential oils to take it to the next level and give you the energy to conquer the day.

8) Fresh OolaTea (Citron Green)

Take the finest green teas from China, add a hint of organic lemon and orange, and you create a delightfully fresh and crisp blend to add balance to your day. The subtle citrus aroma welcomes those looking to explore the benefits of green tea for the first time yet is packed with enough antioxidants to please even the most discerning tea enthusiasts. Add two drops of Lime Vitality essential oil, and you'll create a tea experience that increases fat burning and supports brain health.

9) Boost OolaTea (Berry Brulee)

Sip after sip, indulge yourself with this full-bodied organic black tea that is perfectly balanced with organic strawberries and blackberries. But don't let the sweet aroma and intense dessert flavor fool you. When paired with the recommended Copaiba Vitality essential oil, this handcrafted tea will provide the necessary boost to clear your mind and prepare your body for the tasks at hand. This tea improves cardiovascular endurance and boosts concentration.

10) Marrakesh OolaTea (Moroccan Mint)

Inspired by the cobblestone streets of the Moroccan city of Marrakesh, this organic green tea creates a subtle aroma of mint as you explore this amazing city. Mint is not only in the air, Moroccan Mint tea is woven into the fabric of this vibrant and exotic culture. This invigorating blend includes the highest quality green tea, rolled into small pellets resembling gunpowder and mixed with mint. Add Spearmint Vitality essential oil for a tea experience that will brighten your day and prepare you for the adventure ahead. This tea supports respiratory function and aids in digestion.

You have made it through the OolaTea class! There are two more things I want to pass along before we start on the very last part of this class — something that will aromatically help you with the tension of your day. OolaTea is available as a subscription, where a box conveniently ships to your home each month. As a subscriber you get the new blends first and receive 20 % off on individual orders as you discover your favorites. Teas can also be purchased individually at oolatea.com or on Amazon. There is a tea give back program. The OolaGuys teamed up with ricebowls.org to provide meals to the children they bring into safe houses, many who are trafficked children. Every bag of tea purchased provides one meal to a child in need. For a 50 count, 3 meals are provided.

(Optional video 3: Rice bowl challenge, 30 seconds)

Here's a quick recap — to subscribe, go to oolatea.com. For individual orders, go to oolatea.com or Amazon. To do the 14-day detox, go to oolatea.com/detox.

Let's wrap up the final part of Oola with the OolaGuys — and Sarah — talking about the most powerful tool we have to combat emotions and tension — Young Living essential oils.

(Video 4: OolaGuys and Sarah give a 2-minute preview of the Infused 7 kit; 1 sentence on each of the F's)

There are 7 key areas of your life: Fitness, Finance, Family, Field *(career)*, Faith, Friends, and Fun. By completing the Oola Wheel, you already know your weak points; the areas that could benefit from greater balance. I'm going to pass around all seven oils that match those points in your life, but I want you to truly focus on just one or two of them that you feel you struggle the most with. For the other six oils, just smell them as they go by. For the oil of your weakest point, I want you to drop it in the palm of your hand and take three deep breaths with your hands cupped over your nose.

Crash Course in Oola Oils

Here we go — it's a crash course in Oola oils! This is the first script ever professionally published since the Oola oils were released. The notes are paraphrased from an interview with Gary Young at convention upon their release, the Infused 7 booklet, the OolaGuys and their testimonies and stories behind the oils, and aromatherapy research on the individual oils in the blends. The topical protocol was put together as a collaboration project between Young Living Diamond and Gameplan author, Sarah Harnisch, and Aromatherapist Jen O'Sullivan.

Before we go into the 7 F's, if you truly have a desire to balance and grow your life, it's paramount that you be vulnerable and honest as you identify things that hold you back and that propel you forward. We call those OolaBlockers and OolaAccelerators.

OolaBlockers

If you have ever set a goal in your YL Business, or your life for that matter, and it hasn't come to be, it is very likely being blocked by one of the seven most common OolaBlockers. These are the things that get in the way of the life and business you dream of and deserve:

Fear

Unrealistic fear can paralyze you and prevent you from taking actions that will move you forward. A complete disregard of fear can expose you to risks that can take you down. (Oola, p 102).

Guilt

We all make mistakes, and we all have said and done things that make us feel guilty. Persistent guilt becomes a real OolaBlocker that can really hinder you from the life you want. Experiencing guilt is not a crime. Choosing to carry guilt with you every day is. (Oola, p 108).

Anger

Being persistently or violently angry affects not only you, but everyone around you, and can bring consequences that you will live with forever. If you harbor anger and let it slowly eat away at your soul, it will des your chances for an Oola life. (Oola, p 114).

Self-Sabotage

Subconscious negative self-talk speaks up, you decide that you are not worth it, and you unknowingly begin the process of self-sabotage. (Oola, p 120).

Laziness

Anyone at the top of their game has one thing in common — they are not lazy. They are passionate about their life and worked very hard to get to the top. On the path to Oola, there is no room for lazy. It cannot be part of your life in any way, shape, or form. Lazy blocks Oola. What the lazy want, the disciplined get. (Oola, p 126).

Envy

Envy is worse than jealousy. Jealousy is wanting what others have. Envy is wanting what others have and wanting them not to have it. Envy can suck the joy out of life. (Oola, p 132).

Focus

If you lack focus, you cannot endure what it takes to balance and grow. Focus becomes an OolaBlocker if it takes one of two forms: lack of focus, or misdirected focus. Delayed gratification is very Oola. Focusing on the larger goal will give you the strength you need to sacrifice now to win later. (Oola, p 140).

OolaAccelerators

Now let's take a look at the OolaAccelerators. These are attributes that will help you balance out that wheel. They move you forward faster. When I'm in a place where I'm feeling stuck or discouraged at the juggling, focusing on one of these areas can really help pull me out of a rut.

Gratitude

Be grateful for and love where you are, where you want to go, and where you have been. Be grateful for every part of the journey. Consider the really bad stuff — is it possible to be grateful for losing your job, getting in an accident, or having a sick child? The hidden gifts from these so-called bad things can take months, years, or a lifetime to be revealed. The faster you see the purpose and become truly grateful for the experience, the more the door opens. (Oola, p 150).

Love

Love is the lightning bolt of all OolaAccelerators. It is so powerful! To give and receive love produces passion. (Oola, p 160).

Discipline

Rarely will you find someone who has succeeded in attaining the life of their dreams without a strong work ethic and discipline. Oola is not for the undisciplined. (Oola, p 168).

Integrity

Be wary of stepping over the line, especially the gray line, to speed up the process of ranking. It happens to the best of us. We want it so badly. We use justification to act in a way that is out of integrity to get us to our goals faster. This will catch up with you, and it will end badly. (Oola, p 178).

Passion

If life were a card game, passion is the trump card. If your passion is strong enough, it has the ability to trump many of the OolaBlockers, like fear, anger, and laziness. Tapping into your passion will empower you to overcome. (Oola, p 186).

Humility

It's quiet confidence. Park your ego at the door. You can learn the importance of humility two ways: 1) by practicing it, or 2) the hard way... by living it. Ever heard of pride before the fall? Learn humility or be humbled. Your choice. (Oola, p 194).

Wisdom

Wisdom is more than just knowledge. There are a lot of very smart people who are not wise. Wisdom is unique because it leans heavily on logic, and little on emotion. You can become wise at a young age if you are open to learning from the experiences of others. (Oola, p 202).

What do you do with all of this? We've taken a look at the OolaWheel, and your personal strengths and weaknesses. You know things that will pull you back or push you forward. But how do you balance the seven areas of your life?

There are two steps.

Step 1:

Read the Oola mini book when you get home. It's my gift to you to help with balance. It's loaded with 40 top time management tips pulled from hundreds of books and leaders from around the world.

Step 2:

Utilize the Infused 7 kit. At least once every three months, fill out the OolaWheel again. Set goals. See if you've made progress on your weaknesses. Go to bed at night with Balance on your feet and wake up each morning with Grow in your diffuser. Pick one area where you really need growth and carry that Infused 7 oil with you and use it topically and aromatically using the two protocols we trained on today. Say the affirmations when you apply the oil; it gets your tongue speaking life over the imbalance in your step.

Let's take a closer look at the Infused 7 kit, so you can truly understand the Oola oils. How can an oil help you with fun? Isn't that a little crazy? Not really. Not when you consider what oils can do emotionally for the body. They have naturally occurring chemical constituents that enact emotional change. They are tiny enough to get the emotional center of the brain. It makes sense — people have been using herbs and oils for thousands of years for these exact purposes — even for emotions.

My best advice is to truly try this kit for 21 days and see how you feel at the end of the journey *(for a free 21-day challenge, go to oolalife. com/oolaylchallenge).* If you forget a day, just pick back up where you left off. Get that diffuser going and get these oils on your body. See if you have made improvements in balance and focus and time management. I feel empowered when I use the Oola oils. They have made a huge difference for me. Let's go through the kit.

Fitness:

Your physical health affects everything you do and every area of your life. Fitness is about feeling good, looking good, being healthy and being productive. It is a healthy body and a healthy mind. It's how you move and what you eat. The Fitness blend is specially formulated to uplift, energize, and give you the inspiration to achieve your fitness goals.

Oils in the blend: Cypress, Copaiba, Cistus, Marjoram, Basil, Idaho Blue Spruce, Clary Sage, Peppermint, Black Pepper, Nutmeg, Balsam Fir

Affirmation: I am fit, healthy, disciplined, and strong.

Additional application ideas: Rub a few drops directly on areas that need support before a strenuous workout. Following your workout, apply again to the same area.

From Gary Young: *"When I am making a blend, I first go to 'what is the need'? Because fitness is a big part of my life, and I know how important it is in everyone's life. But I also have listened to enough people over the years complain about the issue when they start to go to the gym or get into an aerobics program or a Pilates program, whatever it is — to start in fitness. I look at what they complain about. Let's face it — most people get into it because they are out of shape. People who are fit don't get into fitness, they are already there. So, when they start, they get aches and pains and sore muscles and cramps. They get discouraged and quit. That was my objective. What can I put together that will eliminate the problems that they will encounter when they start a fitness program? Cypress is for security. Cistus is calming. Basil restores alertness. Peppermint, Black Pepper and Nutmeg are energizing."*

*Fitness tied for first place as OolaSeeker's (Dave) favorite oil of the Infused 7 kit!

Finance:

Debt is not compatible with the OolaLife and is a major stress. Money fights and money stress is the number one reason for divorce in marriages. Start taking steps to improve your finances! Be a good steward of the money the Lord has trusted you with. This blend is formulated to encourage positive emotions and increased feelings of abundance. It brings about clarity and alertness.

Oils in the blend: Frankincense, Orange, Ocotea, Gathering, Clarity, Humility, Balsam Fir, Royal Hawaiian Sandlewood, Citronella

Affirmation: I am financially free and living abundantly.

Additional application ideas: Use Finance on your triceps and forearms before work to help strengthen your motivation.

From Gary Young: *"When I made Finance, I had the experience of 20 plus years with Abundance. I looked at Finance to bring a little more balance into it, having more years of looking at life and people. I really wanted to look at what we needed. One of the things I did in Finance was to go in first with Frankincense. It's a different approach. The reason I did was because we have such a stigmatism about money. There's all this attitude about money being evil. The Bible doesn't say money is evil — it says the lust for it is wrong. I decided to use Frankincense to break through the stigmatism that's been created for years. I put Gathering in to help us to focus and bring all of our thoughts together. When you are looking at improving your finances, if you want a raise in your job or a promotion or a bonus, you want to be focused on what you're doing. I put Humility in because I watch people all the time start to make money, and they change. You don't know who they are. We're not supposed to change with money — we're supposed to become more humble because we have more power. I have watched people who start climbing the ladder of success and no one wants to be around them. I put Orange in because when you're making money, you want to be happy."*

Family:

Family relationships are powerful and complicated! This oil was specifically formatted to support feelings of unconditional love, patience, and respect. This blend helps to uplift, calm the mind, and may help control negative feelings.

Oils in the blend: Inner Child, Lavender, Geranium, Lemon, Jasmine Absolute, Ylang Ylang, Roman Chamomile, Bergamot, Palmarosa, Cardamom, Frankincense, Cedarwood, Pine, and Xiang Mao

Affirmation: I am unconditionally loving, patient, and respectful.

Additional application ideas: use topically on your neck to help with vibrational connections. This will help balance your emotions around others.

From Gary Young: *"This has been my biggest challenge, trying to find balance in my family. I look back over my life, and I see some things I could have done better. But when you are trying to make a living for your family, sometimes you get so dialed into your work that you don't pay attention to the little things that are really important. There was more feeling that went into the development of "Family" than the other blends. I could see Mary, Jacob and Josef when I was making it. I brought all those feelings together. What I reached for first was Inner Child. When we are dialed in to just working, we block everything out because we think it's ok. But we don't stop to think that maybe there is something going on emotionally that we're missing. What helps us to tune in to our kids is our Inner Child and recognizing our inner emotions. Those emotions need to be respected. I put Lavender in next because I wanted to bring balance to it. I didn't want Inner Child to take us too deep. Rose Geranium brings peace. It's good for liver support. When we get angry, we build a lot of toxins in the liver. Ylang Ylang compliments Rose Geranium for the masculine-feminine energy that we have. Cedarwood is a conifer tree that is anchoring and grounding. It also opens us so we can receive more and do more. That means we can open our arms to our family and take them in and keep them under our umbrella of protection. By putting Pine and Cedarwood together you get a balance, so one doesn't overpower the other. Frankincense is for a spiritual anchor. No matter what we do, our faith must be the center."*

*Family is OolaSeeker's *(Dave)* and Sarah's favorite oil of the Infused 7 kit!

Field:

Field is your career or your vocation in life. It's how you spend your day and how you provide, whether it's raising children full time or out in the work force in a cubicle. Many of us aspire to our dream job! The Field blend has been formulated to encourage feelings of self-worth that may help you reach your potential.

Oils in the blend: Cardamom, Frankincense, Present Time, Believe, Ginger, Nutmeg

Affirmation: I am pursuing my purpose in life.

Additional application ideas: Rub a drop on the back of the neck for greater clarity and stimulation. Use this oil as a general pick-me-up during the day. Rub onto muscles before or after a strenuous workout.

From Gary Young: *"You've got people that get up in the morning hating their job. You have people coming home mad because of their attitude or how they were treated, and they bring that home to the family — and the family becomes the recipient of that attitude. Then you have people who don't want to work because of the energy on the job. When I started looking at Field, what does that mean? It means our environment, the total terrain around us. I wanted to start on an oil that works with the brain: Cardamom.*

Frankincense I put underneath the Cardamom. It's so important when I am blending to understand human reaction and the oils, because if I put Frankincense on top, like I did with Finance, then I have a whole different characteristic and function energetically. I laid Frankincense underneath the Cardamom so it was the spiritual base underneath the physical emotions of dealing with life in general. I always want to have a piece of spirituality in there just to keep the perfect balance. Present Time was put in for us to be happy with our family, and job. We have to think forward. We spend too much time thinking about what we did last year. I want people thinking forward by being in the Present Time. When a person wants to improve their life, they have to believe in themselves. You can't empower yourself or improve or step up or live your dream if you don't start believing in yourself. So I put Believe in there."

Faith:

Faith is a complete trust or confidence in God. How you see your place in this world is something you need to explore to attain Oola. The Faith blend is formulated to help you feel grateful, humble, and fully secure in your place in this world.

Oils in the blend: Sacred Frankincense, Balsam Fir, Myrrh, Juniper, Hyssop, Rose, Cedarwood, Sage, Hinoki, Palo Santo, Geranium, Coriander, Bergamot, Lemon, Jasmine Absolute, Ylang Ylang, Roman Chamomile, Palmarosa

Affirmation: I am grateful, humble, and fully connected.

Additional application ideas: Faith is perfect to rub on your wrists or drop one drop on the crown of your head to give you a feeling of being grounded and secure when going into public or to a party where you may be nervous.

From Gary Young: *"It's the same thing with all of my blends. Every time I have a project, or an objective I'm working on, I go back inside myself. I try to put myself in the place of other people. I ask 'what will be the most powerful to stimulate and bring things out*

in a person?' With Faith, we are looking at the oils that were traditionally used by Christ: Frankincense number one, Myrrh number
two, and Balsam oil number three. Even though a lot of people
don't understand, Balsam is the oil that was brought to the Christ
child that was called gold. When we got back to Aramaic translation and the Sanskrit scrolls, it was called liquid gold. When we
went further back in the research, the liquid gold was Balsam
oil. Those three were what was brought to Christ for balancing,
stabilizing, and promoting that feeling of faith, confidence, and
anchoring to the Creator."*

*Faith is OolaGuru's *(Troy)* favorite oil of the Infused 7 kit!

Friends:

A social circle is vital to our well-being. It's important as you advance
in Oola to expand and improve your friend base. Friends has been formulated to encourage feelings of self-worth, empowerment, confidence, and
awareness.

Oils in the blend: Harmony, Lavender, Inner Child, Frankincense,
Blue Cypress, Palo Santo, Xiang Mao.

Affirmation: I am blessed with empowering, healthy friendships

Additional application ideas: Friends is good to rub on the back of
the wrists when you're studying or taking a test.

From Gary Young: *"You want to have something that when you put
it on, everyone will be attracted to you. No matter how hard you've
been working, you still want to smell good. Also — your friends
don't want to be around you if you don't have a good attitude.
What I wanted with Friends was to create the energy of Harmony.
Because everyone has different energy and everyone comes
together, sometimes different personalities bump up against
each other. Harmony helps to just harmonize that and mellow it
out so all personalities can come together without bumping and
clashing. If you get on the Inner Child level, everyone can play.*

With Friends, it's all about association, acceptance, and being in Harmony."

Fun:

Fun is whatever activity or hobby you are personally passionate about. The blend has been formulated to promote uplifting, revitalizing, and euphoric emotions. Its fragrant aroma boosts self-confidence that can enhance the pleasure of pursuing the joys of life.

Oils in the blend: Tangerine, Myrtle, Lemon, Cedarwood, Grapefruit, Spearmint, Nutmeg, Jasmine Absolute

Affirmation: I am pursuing the joys of my life!

Additional application ideas: Rub directly and liberally using a carrier oil on your thighs morning and night. Avoid using in the morning if sun bathing that day. Also used to smooth the skin.

From Gary Young*: "For the oils to make fun, Tangerine, everyone loves the smell of Orange, but Tangerine has more of an exotic fragrance to it, a little more exotic harmony in the frequency that just elevates. Tangerine brings a sense of security. When you are playing, you need support with Nutmeg. Myrtle, you want to have fun. You've got to keep an inner, consistent balance — it's critical."*

You've gone through the entire kit! We're almost done! We mentioned at the beginning that there are three ways of using essential oils: aromatic, topical and internal. We did internal usage with the Vitality line and OolaTea. We discussed an aromatic protocol right at the start of class for all 9 Oola oils. Now, I'm going to wrap up with a topical protocol.

Topical Protocol For The Infused 7 Kit

Place one drop of either Oola Grow or Oola Balance in the palm of your hand. Add three drops of one of the Infused 7 oils on top of it *(the area where you're working hardest).* Make a circular motion in the oil with your fingers. Then apply to these areas in a circular clockwise motion, depending on the oil:

Family: on the neck

Finance: triceps and forearms

Field: back of the neck

Friends: back of the wrists

Faith: crown of the head

Fun: on your thighs

Fitness: on the areas of your body that get sore during a workout

When you are done, cup your hands together, say the affirmation for that oil, and put your hands over your mouth and take three deep breaths. Breathe out twice as slow as you breathe in. If a negative thought comes to mind, say the opposite of it out loud. Take a moment to pray over your day and express gratitude for what the Lord has provided. Then take the remaining oil and put it on your big toes or your 4th and 5th fingers *(that's where the nerve endings come out for your brain),* or rub it into the bottoms of your feet. Never wash your hands! That's wasting oil. You can double the action with aromatic exposure, too, which gets to the limbic lobe of the brain even faster than topical exposure. Put a few drops of an Infused 7 oil in your diffuser and diffuse up to three times a day. The smaller the room, the better. If the scent is too strong, dial back on the number of drops. If you cannot smell it, add more. Stick with the same oil until you notice that there's a different spoke in your wheel that's more out of whack, then switch it up.

Another word for you on emotional use — you may have a good idea of what you want to work on, but sometimes your body will tell you something different. For example, you may be working on your finances for six weeks, but one morning, OolaFamily smells amazing to you. Go with your gut. If you are strongly drawn to an oil, your body has insight and instinct and knows what it wants. Apply that oil that day. You'll supercharge it if you drive it in with Oola Grow or Balance. I like to take it another step and also put a drop of Copaiba on after. Copaiba comes in a Young Living Premium Starter kit and is a fantastic oil for blending.

What Now?

I have one more oil to end with. It's one that's outside the Infused 7 kit. I'm going to put a drop on your hand as you walk out the door, just as a gentle reminder that you can do this! You do not need to walk through every day feeling overwhelmed. You have it in you to take control of your clock and the steps of your day — and to bring it all into balance.

OolaBalance is designed to amplify your ability to focus on passion, behavior, and health. It's a blend of 23 oils to promote calmness and balance. It helps support mental fatigue and balances emotions. It helps you process giving and receiving. It promotes strong relationships. Helps with irritability and to let go of negative feelings. Put a drop just under your pinky finger on the outside bone of your hand and inhale. Take a deep breath and know that you have GOT this. Nothing has a hold on you.

That's the end of our Oola class!

You have a lot to digest! Let's recap. Oola Grow and Oola Balance are for helping you get a leg up on the rhythm of your life. OolaTea is perfectly designed for Vitality oils and is a wonderful way to wean yourself off chemical-laden drinks and detox your system. The Infused 7 kit helps you work on balancing all seven key areas of your life. The Oola mini book will give you more insight and a chance to re-read this script when you get home. You have your OolaWheel filled out and ready to go. And I'm going to hand you an Oola checklist for the next week to keep you on track as you try all of this out. You can print more of these out for future use for free at oolalife.com/gameplan or oilabilityteam.com under *"share" and "Oola"*.

If you're new to oils, how do you get all these blends in your hands? I recommend that you start with a Young Living Premium Starter kit with Desert Mist diffuser. It's where I began my oils journey, it's where I recommend you begin too. I am frugal — and this kit is the only thing on Young

Living's site that's half off! You get a diffuser and 11 full bottles of oil. Then you get 24 % off every order you place — for the rest of your life. Use my referral number, and it will bless my family. Thank you for supporting our family business!

After that, I'd recommend you sign up for Essential Rewards --- and add the Infused 7 kit, and Oola Balance and Oola Grow. That will allow you to implement all that you've learned today. It is the complete Oola package. If you want to try some OolaTea, any Vitality oil you need will be in the same button under Essential Rewards. The benefit to ER is 10 % back immediately, then 20 % back after 4 months, and 25 % back after 25 months. There are also freebies for hitting certain benchmarks of 190, 250, and 300pv. This past month the 300pv order gave me $215 in free oils! It's worth every penny. It is like Christmas every single month. Each month, you pick out new things based on your family's needs. And with every order, you are kicking chemicals to the curb. You are the guardian of the four walls of your home. Protect it.

I have a laptop in the back of the room and would be happy to help you navigate the website. Anyone who signs today will get a free Fearless book and Fearless calendar as a gift, to train you in aromatherapy as you learn how to oil. This was the best decision I've made for my family. I have never looked back. Once you learn to oil, you have a completely different vantage point on how you care for your family.

Make sure you check out the oolalife.com/gameplan website for more Oola freebies — and the oilabilityteam.com/oola website for free audio classes you can listen to on your cell phone. It's digital aromatherapy training that you can do from anywhere.

I want to end today with the whole heart of Oola. There's a powerful story of hope that will encourage you as you start to look at the seven areas of your life, and slowly start to bring them all into balance. It's tough, it takes time and discipline, but the payoff is worth it. Let's end with the Heather Project.

(Video 5: Heather project, 4 minutes)

Thank you for investing in YOU today. I want to leave you with one thought, in honor of Heather. Change starts with a simple commitment. What is the one thing, that if you committed to changing it today, holds the power to completely transform your entire life? That *"one thing"* is called your OolaOne. Start there. Write it down below and read it daily. If it's a large goal, set smaller progressive goals to build momentum on the way to achieving it. You only move from the place where you are if you set goals and take action.

That is the last of this class! I will stay until the last person leaves to answer any questions you may have! You are worth fighting for. Balance and time — it's worth fighting for. Pick an area of weakness - OolaOne - and target it each month. Don't underestimate the power of the oils! Oola is one of the greatest tools I have in my oils arsenal for balance. You have it in you to find purpose, wellness, and abundance. You are loved, you are cherished, and you are Oola!!

Oola For Business Builders Script
"Finding Time for Your Young Living Business"
by Young Living Diamond Sarah Harnisch

Script: 25 minutes, plus 17 minutes of video;
Optional 25 minutes reading time management tips out of this book.

(Prior to class, begin diffusing Oola Grow. Prep your TV or computer to show the five Oola videos. As attendees arrive, hand them an Oola mini and instruct them to turn to the pages of the wheel. Allow 15 minutes to fill out the questionnaire and personal OolaWheels. At the end of class, give them the printable at oolalife.org/gameplan or oilabilityteam.com/oola so they have an Oola system once they leave.)

Hey there! My name is _____ and I am your _____ upline! I'm very excited about this class, because it's one of the top questions I get from business builders — how to find the time. How do you juggle life, home, marriage, a full-time job — and launch a network marketing business?

I think the most powerful thing is knowing your why. Knowing why you are doing this will get you out of bed in the morning and give you cause to keep fighting.

If you've not seen the income disclosure guide, open your Oola mini — the gift I gave you as you came in — and take a peek right now. For most of us, the chance at freedom is enough reason to do this business. If you're brand new and not really sure why you're here — here are a list of the other perks of a Young Living business:

1) Financial Freedom.

The income is beyond our wildest dreams. Network marketing works. It's not a lottery, it's a mathematical certainty. The more you share, the more people fall in love, the larger your organization grows. It's a circle. We do better when we bless those beneath us. I built it with one tool: a love of people.

2) The Timing Has Never Been Better.

People are looking for chemical-free homes. They are reading labels. Large companies are changing their ingredients lists because you are asking for something better. That means you have 100 % market share. You can speak to men and women, kids and the elderly, those with means and those without — because you have what everyone wants: wellness.

3) You Are Your Own Boss And Set Your Own Hours.

Waking up and dictating your own day is very Oola.

4) You Can Take Time Off And Still Get Paid.

How? In network marketing you amass a team. That team is still ordering and still teaching classes whether you are there or not. You're getting paid on that volume whether you show up to the ballgame or not. That means the business is there for you even when you can't always be there for the business. If I don't show up for work, I lose my job. If I miss two weeks of work due to a family emergency, I go two weeks without a paycheck. That doesn't happen when you build a team with Young Living.

5) There Is Willable Income.

That means if something happens to you, and you have written a will, your Young Living income will go to whom you have willed it. This holds the power not only to change your financial future, but the financial legacy for those you love. Forever.

6) Relationships.

The people you meet along the way — your team, your upline, your crossline friends, will change your life for the better. They have the same vision you have: wellness, purpose, and abundance. They are swimming in the same direction. I cannot imagine my life now without the incredible friendships I've been blessed with.

7) Bonuses.

I'm talking all-expenses-paid trips to the farms for Silver, Gold, Platinum and Diamond, separate phone lines for questions, Facebook groups, and all kinds of swag at each rank. Young Living is a generous company.

8) Freedom.

You can't free others when you are in bondage. I loved what I did, but I was chained. Freedom to me is giving generously. It's the ability to dictate your clock and your gifts. It's the chance to truly have balance because you control your life. You can't put a price tag on freedom.

This is a unique class, because we get to learn a Young Living business from the lens of Oola.

What is Oola?

Oola comes from the word *"Ooh la la"*... that's what life feels like when you are happy, balanced, growing and looking forward to what the world has in store for you. Oola is defined as a life that is balanced and growing in the key areas of health, finances, career, relationships and well-being. Oola is the ultimate plan for achieving balance in an unbalanced world.

A few years ago, two guys named Dr. Troy Amdahl (@OolaGuru) and Dr. Dave Braun (@OolaSeeker) penned a book about the seven key areas of your life and how to bring them in balance. That book became an international best seller. They have an audience of over a million people following them as they crisscross the country in their vintage 1970 VW surf bus collecting the dreams of the people they meet in the form of handwritten stickers stuck to the side of the OolaBus. It caught the eye of Young Living, and they partnered with them in 2013 when Gary Young, the founder of Young Living, developed the first Oola oils: Oola Grow and Oola Balance. Let's pass them around right now — take a deep breath from the bottle as it goes by.

Grow:

Oola Grow is a blend of 23 Young Living oils — six of them are not available as singles. This is my favorite oil for courage and to focus on the task at hand. It's my stay-on-track oil to encourage clarity of thought and action, personal growth, happiness and empowerment. Oola Grow promotes feelings of acceptance. It's AMAZING.

Balance:

Oola Balance is designed to amplify your ability to focus on passion, behavior, and health. It's also a blend of 23 oils to promote calmness and balance. It helps support mental fatigue and balances emotions. It helps you process giving and receiving. It promotes strong relationships and helps with irritability and to let go of negative feelings. Put a drop just under your pinky finger on the outside bone of your hand and inhale. Take a deep breath and know that you've GOT this. Nothing has a hold on you.

The neat thing about this class is that we get to pair Oola emotional oils with goal setting, drive, focus, and time management. You'll walk out today feeling empowered and excited about your business. Watch this video with me for a moment as the OolaGuys and Sarah Harnisch, the author of the Oola mini, hang out with us for this training. *(Snag the videos at oolalife.com/gameplan or oilabilityteam.com/oola).*

(Video 1: The OolaGuys and Sarah, 3 minutes: 7 F's of Oola through a business lens)

Let's recap that — the 7 F's of Oola are Fitness, Finance, Family, Field *(career),* Faith, Friends and Fun. Are you in a place where you feel like you are dropping the ball? That you do nothing with excellence, and everything with mediocrity? You are running from fire to fire — with no gameplan or strategy. You don't like where you are, and you see no way out to get where you want to be. That's exactly what this class is all about; training balance.

For the next 15 minutes, open your Oola mini. Inside are questions in all 7 F's. Be completely honest when answering them; this is just between you and you. Then I'll show you how to mark your scores on the OolaWheel so you can see which areas of your life need the most balance.

(Allow 15 minutes for them to answer the questions and fill out the wheel)

The OolaWheel will reveal your low areas; the areas most out of balance right now. That's the part of your life you're most stressing about right now. There are OolaBlockers that will hold you back from bringing them in balance — and there are OolaAccelerators that will propel you toward balance in that area. Let's check in with the OolaGuys and Sarah again — to see how to use these to our advantage when building a Young Living business.

(Video 2: OolaBlockers and OolaAccelerators, 6 minutes)

The average employee only spends 2 hours 53 minutes in a work day... working! That means if you were to put in just a fraction of that time toward your business, you'd explode. The key is consistency — not daily hustle. You can only hustle for so long. But consistency will bring the best results.

The third part of this class is to focus on digging out. You now know your strengths and your weaknesses. Let's talk about how to fix it. For this, I'm going to rely on you guys to do some of the teaching. Sarah Harnisch has amassed the top tips across all of Young Living for time management. They are inside the Oola mini. We're going to take a few minutes and read them top down, as many as you would like, to give you a leg up and some new ideas on how to manage your clock.

(Turn in the Oola mini to "40 Best Time Management Tips for Your Young Living Business". This is several pages of text. You can choose to have different people in the crowd read it, you can read it aloud, you can read just the headline on each paragraph and elaborate with your own stories, or you can highlight the top 5 or 10 and tell them to go home and read the rest of the mini. Do what suits your teaching style best.)

Let me give you the top tips from the Diamonds as they built:

- *give up small pleasures to make way for two hours a week to teach*
- *put your paycheck in my gas tank for 6 months to go where your friends are and share*
- *practice the 3-page Gameplan 101 script and get it in front of anyone that would listen*
- *dial back some of the routines of your day (length of breakfast, etc...) to find more minutes for the business*
- *do income producing activities (teach classes, get people on ER, train your leaders) even when you are tired*
- *ban excuses from your lips*
- *make a commitment to teach classes even when it was hard*
- *schedule 4 classes a month, even if they are only with one person*
- *have self-control to let things go if they are not perfect*
- *be disciplined*

Every day wake up with the three most important things, and when you get to your business hours, focus on only those until you have them done. Make sure you have a class a week on your calendar, even if it's only with one person. That's the number one thing that will grow your team! If all else falls aside because you're in a season of busy, never stop sharing. If I had to pick one income producing activity that will lead to the most growth, it would be teaching classes. You can't find leaders if you're not teaching. You can't get people on Essential Rewards if you are not teaching. It all comes down to the class.

Young Living Diamond Sarah Harnisch has developed a few tools that will help to keep on the straight and narrow if life gets overwhelming.

1) The Gameplanner — this is loaded with the three income producing activities: teaching classes, getting people on ER, and training your leaders. There's Gameplan bootcamp tracking, stat tracking, rank mapping, and more — to get you organized.

2) Textable classes. When people say they don't have time to show up for your class, text them the entire class on their phone to listen to as they drive. They are FREE at oilabilityteam.com under *"share"*.

3) Purple bags. 80 % of your business is simply being prepared. It's having the right tools on hand when conversations arise that could lead to a kit sale. Inside my purple bags, I have a photo of the starter kit, instruction how to order, my contact information, a 101 or Toxin Free Life *(Thieves)* class on audio cd, Fearless *(which trains the lifestyle, not just the kit),* and Your Gameplan — the business opportunity. You can find all the supplies at oilabilityteam.com under *"share"* and *"purple bags".* Many of the tools are free printables.

4) DVD's. If you're too timid to teach, grab the Intro to Young Living DVD at oilabilityteam.com and invite people to your home and play hostess. Or loan the DVD out and check in. It works!

These are all time-savers to help you with frustration!

How do you find the time to teach? How do you balance all the plates in the air? With all the demands on your time, do you ever feel that as a circus performer, running from spinning plate to spinning plate, to try and catch them before they crash and hit the floor? How do you juggle it all without exhaustion?

The secret is there is no secret. It comes down to ten thousand small decisions, discipline, discernment, and self-control. If you can dial back a few areas of your life, not over commit, let a few things go and sacrifice small things to go for the larger goal, and have consistency in your business — those are the greatest tools you'll have in your arsenal to rank up. Most days you'll feel behind. And that's ok! Even the Diamonds feel behind. Just look at your results. If you have OGV growth, you're doing something right. Hustling is great, but you'll get even more results — and results that are long-lasting — if you can run the race with consistency. For Sarah Harnisch, that was a class a week. Four classes a month, or a commitment of 8 hours a month, was what it took for her to build nearly all the way to Platinum. Steady consistency.

The good news is that Gary Young has developed some oils to help you along the way. That's where Oola comes in. First, you fill out the OolaWheel and figure out where your weaknesses are. Then you use oils to specifically hone-in on those areas.

We will spend the last part of this class delving into the Infused 7 kit. Let's turn back to the OolaGuys and Sarah for the backstory on the kit.

(Video 3: Infused 7 Kit; How It Came About, Our Favorites, How to Use It; 5 minutes)

How do you use this incredible kit, so you can truly understand the Oola oils for the first time? How can an oil help you with fun?? Isn't that a little crazy? Not really. Not when you consider what oils can do emotionally for the body. They have naturally occurring chemical constituents that enact emotional change. They are tiny enough to get the emotional center of the brain. It makes sense — people have been using herbs and oils for thousands of years for these exact purposes — even for emotions.

My best advice is to truly try this kit for 21 days and see how you feel at the end of the journey. If you forget a day, just pick back up where you left off. Get that diffuser going and get these oils on your body. See if you have made improvements in balance and focus and time management. I feel empowered when I use the Oola oils. They have made a huge difference for me. Let's go through the kit.

Fitness:

Your physical health affects everything you do and every area of your life. Fitness is about feeling good, looking good, being healthy and being productive. It is a healthy body and a healthy mind. It's how you move and what you eat. The Fitness blend is specially formulated to uplift, energize, and give you the inspiration to achieve your fitness goals.

Oils in the blend: Cypress, Copaiba, Cistus, Marjoram, Basil, Idaho Blue Spruce, Clary Sage, Peppermint, Black Pepper, Nutmeg, Balsam Fir

Affirmation: I am fit, healthy, disciplined, and strong.

Additional application ideas: Rub a few drops directly on areas that need support before a strenuous workout. Following your workout, apply again to the same area.

From Gary Young: *"When I am making a blend, I first go to 'what is the need'? Because fitness is a big part of my life, and I know how important it is in everyone's life. But I also have listened to enough people over the years complain about the issue when they start to go to the gym or get into an aerobics program or a Pilates program, whatever it is—to start in fitness. I look at what they complain about. Let's face it—most people get into it because they are out of shape. People who are fit don't get into fitness, they are already there. So, when they start, they get aches and pains and sore muscles and cramps. They get discouraged and quit. That was my objective. What can I put together that will eliminate the problems that they will encounter when they start a fitness program? Cypress is for security. Cistus is calming. Basil restores alertness. Peppermint, Black Pepper and Nutmeg are energizing."*

Finance:

Debt is not compatible with the OolaLife and is a major stress. Money fights and money stress is the number one reason for divorce in marriages. Start taking steps to improve your finances! Be a good steward of the money the Lord has trusted you with. This blend is formulated to encourage positive emotions and increased feelings of abundance. It brings about clarity and alertness.

Oils in the blend: Frankincense, Orange, Ocotea, Gathering, Clarity, Humility, Balsam Fir, Royal Hawaiian Sandlewood, Citronella

Affirmation: I am financially free and living abundantly.

Additional application ideas: Use Finance on your triceps and forearms before work to help strengthen your motivation.

From Gary Young: *"When I made Finance, I had the experience of 20 plus years with Abundance. I looked at Finance to bring a little more balance into it, having more years of looking at life and people. I really wanted to look at what we needed. One of the things I did in Finance was to go in first with Frankincense. It's a different approach. The reason I did was because we have such a stigmatism about money. There's all this attitude about money being evil. The Bible doesn't say money is evil — it says the lust for it is wrong. I decided to use Frankincense to break through the stigmatism that's been created for years. I put Gathering in to help us to focus and bring all of our thoughts together. When you are looking at improving your finances, if you want a raise in your job or a promotion or a bonus, you want to be focused on what you're doing. I put Humility in because I watch people all the time start to make money, and they change. You don't know who they are. We're not supposed to change with money--we're supposed to become more humble because we have more power. I have watched people who start climbing the ladder of success and no one wants to be around them. I put Orange in because when you're making money, you want to be happy."*

Family:

Family relationships are powerful and complicated! This oil was specifically formatted to support feelings of unconditional love, patience, and respect. This blend helps to uplift, calm the mind, and may help control negative feelings.

Oils in the blend: Inner Child, Lavender, Geranium, Lemon, Jasmine Absolute, Ylang Ylang, Roman Chamomile, Bergamot, Palmarosa, Cardamom, Frankincense, Cedarwood, Pine, and Xiang Mao

Affirmation: I am unconditionally loving, patient, and respectful.

Additional application ideas: use topically on your neck to help with vibrational connections. This will help balance your emotions around others.

From Gary Young: *"This has been my biggest challenge, trying to find balance in my family. I look back over my life, and I see some things I could have done better. But when you are trying to make a living for your family, sometimes you get so dialed into your work that you don't pay attention to the little things that are really important. There was more feeling that went into the development of "Family" than the other blends. I could see Mary, Jacob and Josef when I was making it. I brought all those feelings together. What I reached for first was Inner Child. When we are dialed in to just working, we block everything out because we think it's ok. But we don't stop to think that maybe there is something going on emotionally that we're missing. What helps us to tune in to our kids is our Inner Child and recognizing our inner emotions. Those emotions need to be respected. I put Lavender in next because I wanted to bring balance to it. I didn't want Inner Child to take us too deep. Rose Geranium brings peace. It's good for liver support. When we get angry, we build a lot of toxins in the liver. Ylang Ylang compliments Rose Geranium for the masculine-feminine energy that we have. Cedarwood is a conifer tree that is anchoring and grounding. It also opens us so we can receive more and do more. That means we can open our arms to our family and take them in and keep them under our umbrella of protection. By putting Pine and Cedarwood together you get a balance, so one doesn't overpower the other. Frankincense is for a spiritual anchor. No matter what we do, our faith must be the center."*

Field:

Field is your career or your vocation in life. It's how you spend your day and how you provide, whether it's raising children full time or out in the work force in a cubicle. Many of us aspire to our dream job! The Field blend has been formulated to encourage feelings of self-worth that may help you reach your potential.

Oils in the blend: Cardamom, Frankincense, Present Time, Believe, Ginger, Nutmeg

Affirmation: I am pursuing my purpose in life.

Additional application ideas: Rub a drop on the back of the neck for greater clarity and stimulation. Use this oil as a general pick-me-up during the day. Rub onto muscles before or after a strenuous workout.

From Gary Young: *"You've got people that get up in the morning hating their job. You have people coming home mad because of their attitude or how they were treated, and they bring that home to the family — and the family becomes the recipient of that attitude. Then you have people who don't want to work because of the energy on the job. When I started looking at Field, what does that mean? It means our environment, the total terrain around us. I wanted to start on an oil that works with the brain: Cardamom. Frankincense I put underneath the Cardamom. It's so important when I am blending to understand human reaction and the oils, because if I put Frankincense on top, like I did with Finance, then I have a whole different characteristic and function energetically. I laid Frankincense underneath the Cardamom so it was the spiritual base underneath the physical emotions of dealing with life in general. I always want to have a piece of spirituality in there just to keep the perfect balance. Present Time was put in for us to be happy with our family, and job. We have to think forward. We spend too much time thinking about what we did last year. I want people thinking forward by being in the Present Time. When a person wants to improve their life, they have to believe in themselves. You can't empower yourself or improve or step up or live your dream if you don't start believing in yourself. So I put Believe in there."*

Faith:

Faith is a complete trust or confidence in God. How you see your place in this world is something you need to explore to attain Oola. The Faith blend is formulated to help you feel grateful, humble, and fully secure in your place in this world.

Oils in the blend: Sacred Frankincense, Balsam Fir, Myrrh, Juniper, Hyssop, Rose, Cedarwood, Sage, Hinoki, Palo Santo, Geranium, Coriander, Bergamot, Lemon, Jasmine Absolute, Ylang Ylang, Roman Chamomile, Palmarosa

Affirmation: I am grateful, humble, and fully connected.

Additional application ideas: Faith is perfect to rub on your wrists or drop one drop on the crown of your head to give you a feeling of being grounded and secure when going into public or to a party where you may be nervous.

From Gary Young: *"It's the same thing with all of my blends. Every time I have a project, or an objective I'm working on, I go back inside myself. I try to put myself in the place of other people. I ask 'what will be the most powerful to stimulate and bring things out in a person?' With Faith, we are looking at the oils that were traditionally used by Christ: Frankincense number one, Myrrh number two, and Balsam oil number three. Even though a lot of people don't understand, Balsam is the oil that was brought to the Christ child that was called gold. When we got back to Aramaic translation and the Sanskrit scrolls, it was called liquid gold. When we went further back in the research, the liquid gold was Balsam oil. Those three were what was brought to Christ for balancing, stabilizing, and promoting that feeling of faith, confidence, and anchoring to the Creator."*

Friends:

A social circle is vital to our well-being. It's important as you advance in Oola to expand and improve your friend base. Friends has been formulated to encourage feelings of self-worth, empowerment, confidence, and awareness.

Oils in the blend: Harmony, Lavender, Inner Child, Frankincense, Blue Cypress, Palo Santo, Xiang Mao.

Affirmation: I am blessed with empowering, healthy friendships

Additional application ideas: Friends is good to rub on the back of the wrists when you're studying or taking a test.

From Gary Young: *"You want to have something that when you put it on, everyone will be attracted to you. No matter how hard you've been working, you still want to smell good. Also — your friends don't want to be around you if you don't have a good attitude. What I wanted with Friends was to create the energy of Harmony. Because everyone has different energy and everyone comes together, sometimes different personalities bump up against each other. Harmony helps to just harmonize that and mellow it out so all personalities can come together without bumping and clashing. If you get on the Inner Child level, everyone can play. With Friends, it's all about association, acceptance, and being in Harmony."*

Fun:

Fun is whatever activity or hobby you are personally passionate about. The blend has been formulated to promote uplifting, revitalizing, and euphoric emotions. Its fragrant aroma boosts self-confidence that can enhance the pleasure of pursuing the joys of life.

Oils in the blend: Tangerine, Myrtle, Lemon, Cedarwood, Grapefruit, Spearmint, Nutmeg, Jasmine Absolute

Affirmation: I am pursuing the joys of my life!

Additional application ideas: Rub directly and liberally using a carrier oil on your thighs morning and night. Avoid using in the morning if sun bathing that day. Also used to smooth the skin.

From Gary Young: *"For the oils to make fun, Tangerine, everyone loves the smell of Orange, but Tangerine has more of an exotic fragrance to it, a little more exotic harmony in the frequency that just elevates. Tangerine brings a sense of security. When you are playing, you need support with Nutmeg. Myrtle, you want to have fun. You've got to keep an inner, consistent balance — it's critical."*

You've gone through the entire kit! We're almost done! We mentioned at the beginning that there are three ways of using essential oils: aromatic, topical and internal. We did internal usage with the Vitality line and OolaTea. We discussed an aromatic protocol right at the start of class for all 9 Oola oils. Now, I'm going to wrap up with a topical protocol.

Topical protocol for the Infused 7 Kit

Place one drop of either Oola Grow or Oola Balance in the palm of your hand. Add three drops of one of the Infused 7 oils on top of it *(the area where you're working hardest)*. Make a circular motion in the oil with your fingers. Then apply to these areas in a circular clockwise motion, depending on the oil:

Family: on the neck

Finance: triceps and forearms

Field: back of the neck

Friends: back of the wrists

Faith: crown of the head

Fun: on your thighs

Fitness: on the areas of your body that get sore during a workout

When you are done, cup your hands together, say the affirmation for that oil, and put your hands over your mouth and take three deep breaths. Breath out twice as slow as you breathe in. If a negative thought comes to mind, say the opposite of it out loud. Take a moment to pray over your day and express gratitude for what the Lord has provided. Then take the remaining oil and put it on your big toes or your 4th and 5th fingers *(that's where the nerve endings come out for your brain)* or rub it into the bottoms of your feet. Never wash your hands! That's wasting oil. You can double the action with aromatic exposure, too, which gets to the limbic lobe of the brain even faster than topical exposure. Put a few drops of an Infused 7 oil in your diffuser and diffuse up to three times a day. The smaller the room, the better. If the scent is too strong, dial back on the number of drops. If you cannot smell it, add more. Stick with the same oil until you notice that there's a different spoke in your wheel that's more out of whack, then switch it up.

Another word for you on emotional use — you may have a good idea of what you want to work on, but sometimes your body will tell you something different. For example, you may be working on your finances for six weeks, but one morning, OolaFamily smells amazing to you. Go with your gut. If you are strongly drawn to an oil, your body has insight and instinct and knows what it wants. Apply that oil that day. You'll supercharge it if you drive it in with Oola Grow or Balance. I like to take it another step and also put a drop of Copaiba on after. Copaiba comes in a Young Living Premium Starter kit and is a fantastic oil for blending.

Once the oils are on your body, write down three simple business goals on a 3x5 card and tackle them every day! Don't allow yourself pleasures like social media until those three tasks are done.

We've hit on the top time management tips, the 7 F's, the OolaWheel, Oola Blockers and OolaAccelerators — and now, an emotional way of tackling all your feelings while you go home and start to juggle all those plates. Let's check in with the OolaGuys and Sarah one last time...

(Video 4: A Word of Encouragement, 3 minutes)

You have what it takes to go all the way in Young Living. Running a business is not easy, but it is worth it. The little bits you invest right now have the power to change your future and leave a legacy for your family — if only you will walk.

Let's Review What To Do:

1) Wake up with your why in your head.

2) Tackle three income-producing business activities each day.

3) Schedule one class a week, even if it's with a single person.

4) Every month or so, re-do your wheel so you know where your time must go.

5) Make sure you're Oola oiling with intent every day, based on the results of your wheel.

6) Speak life over yourself! Don't allow doubt or excuses in your head.

Your homework assignment is to go home and read the Oola mini. Highlight the top five things that spoke to you and implement them. Get inspired. Take the free Oola for Business printable *(oolalife.com/game-plan or oilabilityteam.com)* and use it to hold yourself accountable to Oola for a week. If you are faithful with the small things, the Lord will make you ruler over more. Own your clock — don't let it own you.

Change starts with a simple commitment. What is the one thing, that if you committed to changing it today, holds the power to completely transform your entire life. That *"one thing"* is called your OolaOne. Write it down below and read it daily. If it's a large goal, set smaller progressive goals to build momentum on the way to achieving it. You only move from the place where you are if you set goals and take action.

BONUS

You may be asking yourself — is all this worth the climb? Is it worth the work? It is worth every drop. See yourself crossing things off your bucket list. Envision yourself debt free. You have a hope and a future ahead of you, if you will walk the road it takes to get there.

Know who you are! You are a DIAMOND RISING. And you are Oola.

Freedom is on the other side. Go fight for it.

For 21 days of challenges to help you meet your goals, check out oolalife.com/ oolaylchallenge

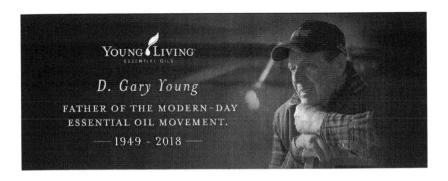

In Memoriam

D. Gary Young: The Father of the Modern Essential Oils Movement

1949-2018

By Sarah Harnisch

D. Gary Young, the founder of Young Living Essential Oils, has changed the entire course of my life. I am a name in a sea of people he has impacted for the better. How do you write a tribute to a man who plucked you from poverty? Who has changed the way you care for your kids? Who has shifted your job description to a hope-bringer? Who has caused you to dream bigger? I have new focus because of what Gary has given to me. And I will shout his message from every mountain top until the last breath in my lungs is gone. I will write it in a hundred more books. Gary Young IS wellness, purpose, and abundance.

There are dozens of stories I could share with you about my time with Gary: when I met him in Venice on the Global Leadership Cruise to Venice, our 30 minute conversation in the hallways of Beauty School in Utah, my interviews with him in Hawaii for the Drive to Win, the moments on stage with him last year getting my Diamond award—when he walked right past me and wrapped his arms around my littlest son, Noah, and poured wisdom into his ear right on the stage as a

* D. Gary Young banner image used by permission from Young Living Essential Oils.

packed room waited. They waited on a ten-year-old at a Diamond gala, because to Gary, every person has value. This is a man who loved people. People were his soul. And so I will start and end with Gary's vision and legacy, in the hopes that if you are picking up this book and did not have the chance to meet him personally, you will be inspired to carry on his work. It does not matter if you've not seen him face to face. Do not feel a loss. Gary Young is not gone. He's inside you, inside me, and inside the millions of lives he's changed with his vision, his heart, and his raw love. He will always see the best in you, no matter what.

Right after Gameplan's release, I felt a strong prompting that Gary should read the book. It had nothing to do with me, it was just meant to be an encouragement to him that we as leaders had captured his purpose and would spend our lives sharing. Doc Oli Wenker, who wrote the forward to this 2nd edition, is a close friend of mine, and Gary's personal physician. Gary had stayed at his home last year, and I sent a copy of Gameplan to Oli to give to him as a gift.

I took some time to write a note to say thank you for all he'd done for me. I told Gary if I could sum up Young Living in a single word, I'd pick "freedom." Because of what I had learned from Gary, I would spend the rest of my life bringing freedom to people on my team—financial freedom, relational freedom, mental freedom, spiritual freedom, emotional freedom—freedom in every sense of the word. My tears were on the page, tears of gratefulness, as I slipped that book in the mail.

A month or two later, Ellen, Oli's wife, wrote me, and said Gary had been given the book—and stayed up the entire night reading Gameplan. At convention in 2017 a few months later, he stood on stage in a workshop and said he'd been given a note from a leader—and then cited four sentences from memory, word for word, of the letter I'd written inside that book. It impacted me in the deepest way that those words would mean something to Gary Young.

Gary's dreams have always been so much bigger than mine! It is precious to me to know, in the smallest way, that he did have a moment to realize the gratitude that one family has for him. We can never repay what we have been given: generational wealth, purpose, friendships, and a total change in vision.

Gary was never silent about his purpose. He mentioned it every single time I saw him. He wanted "to get oils in every home in the world." My challenge to you is to make that happen. Make it your goal THIS YEAR to rank up in Young Living. Do it for Gary.

Why?

Because with every rank, your team grows larger. That's getting oils in every home! With every new rank, you get a front row seat to watch hope and freedom duplicated among your leaders. And you carry the torch for Gary Young. This is the man that slept on cold distillery floors in France and hand-drew diagrams of distilleries, then came back to the United States with lavender seeds in his boots and did it better. This is the man that traded what little he had so he could buy land for the first lavender farm. He is always the first to arrive and the last to leave a day of work. This is the man that built distilleries in Canada in minus 80-degree temperatures to make sure Valor oil could return. This is the man that fought physical pain at tremendous cost so he could be here. He loved his family, he loved the corporate staff, and he loved every single Young Living distributor. Even if he has not met you, he knows you. You have the spirit of Young Living inside you. If you could have a conversation with Gary right now, he would have cried with you, told you it was his "leaky eye syndrome", and reminded you to fight harder for your dreams.

It's time for you to pick up where he left off. It's all on our shoulders now! If you think you cannot make a difference—that's exactly what I thought when I got my kit in 2014. Network marketing is not about one person doing it all. It's about many people doing a little. My team spans several continents and several thousand people. But it all started with a single yes, a few friends on a couch at a class in my living room, and passion. It's Gary's passion that keeps me going. I'm going to start another hashtag campaign, because I want you to use it every time you hit a new rank. Know that with every starter kit, another family's lives have been changed, just as yours and mine are. Don't just sit on the blessing you have been given. Share it. Love people as much as Gary did. You have it in you to be a Royal Crown Diamond. Catch the vision and move.

-Sarah Harnisch
#doitforgary #becauseofgary

What's Next?

We've created two awesome printables to help keep you on track with managing your time.

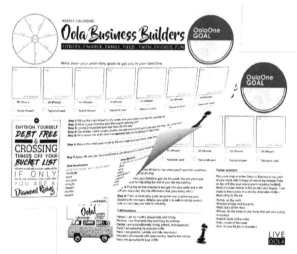

Get yours today!

Save on OolaTea

Save $10 on your first OolaTea monthly subscription box with the promo code: **save10**.

Subscribe today:
www.oolatea.com/subscription

Free Shipping

Receive free shipping on orders over $100 at the OolaStore with the promo code: **liveoola**.

Shop now:
www.oolalife.com/store

Infused 7 Kit

Order your Oola Inspired Young Living essential oils today and start pursuing a life of less stress and more balance.

Learn more:
www.youngliving.com/en_US/products/infused-7